The Nameless
& The Faceless
Women of the Civil War

A Collection of Poems & Essays

LISA G. SAMIA

DESTINY WHISPERS PUBLISHING, LLC
TUCSON, ARIZONA
WWW.DESTINYNOVELS.COM

Copyright © 2021 by Destiny Whispers Publishing, LLC
First Edition, April 14, 2021

"THE NAMELESS & THE FACELESS WOMEN OF THE CIVIL WAR"
LISA G. SAMIA, Author
Destiny Whispers Publishing, LLC
ISBN-13 # 978-1-943504-36-7

Leslie D. Stuart, Creative Director and Executive Editor
Destiny Whispers Publishing, LLC
www.DestinyNovels.com

Some photographs within this collection were taken on location by the author, Lisa G. Samia, and cannot be used or reprinted without written permission. www.LisaSamia.com

The front cover is of Elvira Finch Moore from the author's own photos. Back cover photo is a collage of family heirlooms.

"Our Rose of Remembrance," and "The Flowers of Hope" illustrations are used to symbolize the hardships of the Civil War were created by Shannon A. Reedy; exclusive use, all rights reserved.

All original artwork is property of the illustrator, exclusive permission given for Destiny Whispers Publishing, LLC, all rights reserved.

Destiny Whispers Publishing, LLC
Leslie D. Stuart, Owner
1618 W. Niatross Place
Tucson, AZ 85704
www.DestinyNovels.com

Contents

Introduction
From the Author Lisa G. Samia

The Nameless and the Faceless Women of the Civil War is a collection of 28 poems and 28 essays, along with historical images and personal photos.

This is my second book in the series.

The inspiration for this collection comes from the very first poem and essay about Elvira Finch Moore. She was a relative who was from upstate New York and married John L. Moore in 1853 in Fairfax County, Virginia. This was nine years before the start of the American Civil War. Family history and stories of Elvira suggested she was a traitor, but was she a traitor to the North? The South? We do not know.

Recently, the family discovered Guards and Pickets passes that had been given to Elvira in 1863-1864. The passes show her coming from Fairfax and going to Washington D.C., but in what capacity? We have rumors and legends passed down through the family, but no definitive answers.

Elvira and the mystery that surrounds her life is the inspiration for this collection.

The Nameless and the Faceless Women of the Civil War is about those unrecognized women of that era. Many are without a name or a face, but here they have a voice. As we know, not everyone who experienced the Civil War made it into the history books. Through the rhyme and narrative of poetry, I hope to share their stories, as never before seen or heard.

For example, the narrator in one poem is the voice of a soldier who is writing to his wife. Another features a woman who is nursing an injured soldier.

A particularly moving poem gives a voice to an unnamed theatre attendee, a woman who bears witness to the events at Ford's Theater on April 14, 1865.

Others are civilians who are telling their story of what it was like to be at Gettysburg listening to President Abraham Lincoln present the Gettysburg Address in November 1863 or witnessing the burning of Richmond, Virginia in April 1865.

Here, we bear witness and recognize women, such as the first Black woman to enlist in the Union Army, who was only able to serve while in disguise as a man.

The essays are the factual representations as provided by history, along with author insights. The poems are voices of those who are sharing their stories.

While many of the poems are filled with moments of grief and despair, throughout the collection is a subliminal thread of hope. The lines of North and South are blurred in this collection the reason simply being that suffering has no boundaries.

To my husband, Jim

Carte de Visite for Elvira Finch Moore
Author's own photo, undated

Elvira Finch Moore

My name is Elvira Finch Moore, if you must know
Came to Fairfax in fifty-two for my beau
And married him in fifty-three
The love of my life was all I could see
And left my home in New York, it is to state
Was called a Northerner it was my fate
And I watched as the country did divide
Civil War, North and South, how I cried
That my family life was forever changed
Rebel or Union it was not the same
Heard the whispers from those who did not care
Traitor spy it was my cross to bear
So I ask what you would have done
To help your family from awaiting guns
And cross the Yankee line to seek
Food and supplies I could not be meek
And so now the years did pass away
I am gone from Earth in another place
And still I hear the words traitor spy
Can you help me please, to dispel the lie?
For I ask you once again
What would you have done, my friend
To save your family from the horror of war
I am. I am. Elvira Finch Moore

The Mystery of
Elvira Finch Moore

(1826-1903)

The inspiration for this poem, "Elvira Finch Moore" and for the entire collection, "The Nameless and the Faceless Women of the Civil War," originated from my research and connection to a relative on my husband's side of the family.

The mystery of Elvira Finch Moore is steeped in the family's history with unanswered questions about whether or not Elvira was a Civil War traitor or a spy.

Behind the framed photo of Elvira, which is featured on the cover of this book, is a secret pocket which contains Civil War Guards and Pickets passes. These passes permitted Elvira to move between her home in Fairfax, Virginia and Washington D.C. from 1863-1864.

Much speculation occurred regarding the purpose of her travels. Her story and legend becomes very interesting as we look into the history and movements of Elvira and her husband John L. Moore during the Civil War.

In searching for the true story of Elvira Finch Moore, we begin where she was born in Otsego County, New York (near Cooperstown) in the year 1826. Her father was Judge Lewis Finch. She was the great granddaughter of Captain Peter Low who served with General Washington and he was present with Washington as they crossed the Delaware.

Elvira relocated to Virginia in 1852 and in 1853 she married John L. Moore of Fairfax County. There is no existing family documentation indicating as to why Elvira left New York and her family there, or how she and John initially met.

John L. Moore, the oldest of 13 children, was born in 1828 to William Halley Moore and Mary Ann Blackburn of Fairfax County.

In searching to find out the truth behind the mystery of Elvira's travels, we look to her husband John to see if any clues emerge from his correspondence. We know from family letters that John was more than likely a land and property owner.

In a family letter dated February 10, 1861 from Fairfax County, he writes to his brother and sister:

"Probably you think it strange that the abolition of slavery in Washington would be fatal to us; it would be in this way that; our servants would run away and go there and be secreted there by the free Negroes and the abolitionists of that place."

A suggestion here is that perhaps John and Elvira were slave holders. No evidence has been found that John was a soldier either in the Union or with the Confederacy. Did he pay for a substitute? Was he exempt due to the possibly of owning more than 20 slaves, inherited from his father?

A contradiction begins to emerge as per the Ordinance of Secession from Vienna, Virginia that occurred on May 23, 1861 in which John L. Moore voted against secession, whereas his youngest brother Jeremiah voted for it.

Jeremiah joined the Confederacy and was killed during the war. Vienna was one of three jurisdictions in Fairfax County that voted against secession. There were many Quakers and Northerners in the area who did not agree with secession.

What changed in John's mind from February 1861 to May of 1861? More questions than answers have evolved in this family's story as more information continues to come to light.

In a box full of the Moore-Finch family records I also found a letter that was written by Elvira to her sister in New York talking about her wedding day. The letter was addressed from Peach Grove, (now known as Tyson's Corner) Virginia on October 23, 1853 and it contained a piece of her wedding veil. It was humbling to read this particular letter; some pages looked as if they hadn't been disturbed in over 160 years.

In my quest and zeal to discover the truth of Elvira, the questions about her being a traitor or a spy began to diminish, as I read the words of a woman in love, eager to share her joy and excitement and the beauty of her wedding day with her beloved sister.

Elvira writes about going to Washington D.C. to be married to Mr. Moore. She tells her sister of her wedding bonnet and the satin ribbons around it, so like the one she too wore on her wedding day. It was an extraordinary moving moment exchanged between two sisters.

The discovery of this particular letter binds me even further to this family, as the engagement ring I have worn for the last 32 years once belonged to Elvira's granddaughter, Adarla.

Carte de Visite's (left to right) of Erastus C. Weaver who was Elvira's brother-in law and a Union solider. In the center is her son Millard with the undated photo of Elvira.
Author's own photos

Historians find and painstakingly document the stories of our past, but they don't always explore the deeper meaning of the words that are defining the story.

As a poet that is what I do.

This all seems so very complicated, or maybe it's just as simple as the act of bringing a family member's story to light 150 years after the Civil War. It is for this reason this book is dedicated to her.

In this poem we hear Elvira sharing her story but NOT her whole story. The cover of this book is Elvira's portrait in an undated earlier lithograph. Her expression reveals nothing; if anything, her stoic calm only serves to deepen the mystery that surrounds her.

I am not sure there will ever be a definitive conclusion to this family mystery. Her secrets and her reasons remain her own. More research needs to be done, perhaps by researching the history of other families who Elvira may have known or people she may have influenced by her words and deeds.

However, it is because of the mystery and furtive secrets that surround Elvira and to all those unknown women of the Civil War that compels this book forward.

Here is where for the first time, through my imagination and through facts of history that the unknown voices of women not heard from before can come forth to tell their stories of suffering, sacrifice and survival. Listen to their voices as the humanity of history comes alive.

The view of Gettysburg from Seminary Ridge

All Ye of Gettyburg, Rise

I could not stand it just one moment more
As the rage of battle ceased outside my door
And after three days I tell you now
My eyes gazed upon the carnage I do avow
My family's farm once lush and green
With the fruits of God's blessing it was to be seen
The front acreage that beaconed the eye
Was littered with the dead could not even cry
For in each direction I do state
The dead lay everywhere it was our fate
I could only try to understand you see
The casualties of war that fought to free
All those bounds in chains with no rights
The dead lay here with no one in sight
To die for one's country for a higher cause
Beyond the Union it gave me pause
Yet here lie so many what can I do?
Who are they I ask to bid adieu
For Gettysburg they came and fought and died
There must be more to God I cried
And so I stood among the throng of those
Who gave their lives it must be told
And so I raised my arms to heaven above
And cried to God of whom is love
Rise up all ye of Gettysburg, rise
And take your place along God's side
And ne'er will your bodies be broken and in pain
As you ascent to the heavens in God's reign
For in your sacrifice upon these fields as I roam
You have earned your place in heaven,
Ascend my brethren, to your throne

The Battle of Gettysburg
July 1-3, 1863

    The Battle of Gettysburg was not only the bloodiest of all the battles of the Civil War, but it would in fact become the last time Confederate General Robert E. Lee would fight on Northern soil. It was considered the high water mark of the Confederacy.

    The early campaigns of the Civil War found many Confederate victories at the hands of General Robert E. Lee. This was achieved by outsmarting his opponents by strategically appearing to have greater numbers than the Union Army and also by taking long chances to secure victory.

    This formula was a success with the aid of the equally brilliant General Stonewall Jackson. However, Lee's brilliant tactician lost his life at the Confederate victory at Chancellorsville, Virginia in May of 1863. The loss of General Jackson was one in which Lee would never recover. Yet, fresh from victory at Chancellorsville, Lee took his great army North, thinking the Army of Northern Virginia was invincible.

    This belief, however, would end on the bloody fields of Gettysburg. For three days upon the farmlands of Gettysburg the great Army of Northern Virginia led by General Robert E. Lee and the Army of the Potomac led by General George G. Meade would rage upon each other from July 1-3, 1863.

    This became a decisive Union victory and arguably the turning point in the Civil War. The casualty numbers were staggering with a total of 28,000 for the Confederacy and 23,000 from the Union. The war would rage for two more bloody years. Battle after battle would yield thousands of dead, wounded or missing soldiers.

    For the citizens of Gettysburg, the agony and devastation in the aftermath of the battle is evident in this poem as we hear from an unknown woman. She has emerged from the sanctuary of her home after hearing the ceasefire of battle after three horrifying days.

When she opens her door, the field in front of her is littered with the dead and dying. Soon homes, farms and even churches were used as hospitals to collect the wounded and the dead of both Union and Confederate. As she walks among the battle-torn soldiers it is to God whom she lifts her arms and heart, as if to gather up the souls and help them rise to the Almighty.

Battle of Gettysburg (days two and three)
from Tillie Pierce:

As her friends baked bread with her neighbor on the second day of battle, Tillie Pierce helped distribute that bread to hungry Union troops, but even that seemingly simple task was not without risk.

"It was shortly before noon that I observed soldiers lying on the ground just back of the house, dead. They had fallen just where they had been standing when shot. I was told that they had been picked off by Rebel sharpshooters who were up in Big Round Top.

Toward the middle of the afternoon heavy cannonading began on the two Round Tops just back of the house. This was so terrible and severe that it was with great difficulty we could hear ourselves speak. It began very unexpectedly; so much so, that we were all terror-stricken, and hardly knew what to do....

Those who are familiar with this battle now know what havoc and destruction were accomplished on this afternoon, on the west side of the Round Tops, at Devil's Den, Sherby's Peach Orchard and the Wheat-field." [1]

Similar heartbreaking scenes occurred on such battlefields as Antietam, Fredericksburg, Chancellorsville and Cold Harbor.

Having stood on the battle grounds of Gettysburg and in the stillness and the quiet, I can almost hear the lost cries of those unknown souls whispering in the wind. The most hallowed of all places. The most revered of all places. The most heart wrenching of all places.

A place called Gettysburg.

Wedding day photo from April 1893
Millard J. Moore (Elvira's son) and his bride, Jessie Moore
Author's own photo

Bailey's Crossroads

I came here to Bailey's Crossroads this fine November morn
With my husband to see General McLellan, as his troops adorn
In resplendent marches and grand reviews
The Union Army I never knew
Such grandeur that brought tears to my eyes
As the finery passed me in endless surprise
In rows and columns in precision they hailed
To preserve our Union our President prevailed
As we stood there all of us you see
The President and Congress it was to be
My pride for my Union and love of the sight
Of the marching soldiers so ready to fight
You see this memory has burned into my mind
I knew I was witnessing history sublime
That night after a sleep that would not come
I rose from my bed and slowly begun
The poem in words that echoed my heart
Of those to glory and yet to part
And so it began and forever refrained
My pencil stopping and starting in the strain
And out came these words that flowed from my heart
Listen to them please as I start
'Mine eyes have seen the glory of the coming of the Lord
He is trampling out the vintage
Where the grapes of wrath are stored'
I continued to write my love of the day's earlier sight
Early into the morn no sleep that night
And hope and pray that these words will live
In the heart of liberty and the willingness to forgive

Julia Ward Howe

(1819-1910)
Writing the Battle Hymn of the Republic

Julia Ward Howe of Boston, Massachusetts and her husband Samuel were invited to Washington D.C. in November 1861 by President Abraham Lincoln in appreciation for their devoted work with the Sanitary Commission.

While there, Julia and Samuel visited the Union Army Camp stationed across the Potomac in Fairfax County, Virginia (Bailey's Crossroads) where Union General George McClellan, the head of the Army of the Potomac presided over a grand review of his troops. Also in attendance was President Abraham Lincoln.

While some 70,000 troops marched past the reviewing stand, they began to sing the song (both sung by the North and the South), one in defense of John Brown (Harper's Ferry) and one song celebrating his death, by hanging: "John Brown's body lies a'mouldering in his grave."

Present at the review was a clergyman, James Freeman Clarke, who was familiar with the poetry of Julia Ward Howe. He urged her to write a new song and she describes how that event occurred:

"I replied that I had often wished to do so.... In spite of the excitement of the day I went to bed and slept as usual, but awoke the next morning in the gray of the early dawn, and to my astonishment found that the wished-for lines were arranging themselves in my brain. I lay quite still until the last verse had completed itself in my thoughts, then hastily arose, saying to myself, I shall lose this if I don't write it down immediately. I searched for an old sheet of paper and an old stub of a pen which I had had the night before, and began to scrawl the lines almost

without looking, as I learned to do by often scratching down verses in the darkened room when my little children were sleeping. Having completed this, I lay down again and fell asleep, but not before feeling that something of importance had happened to me."1

Her inspiration of that day's events was the poem, "Battle Hymn of the Republic," which would become the anthem song of the North.

Even with all that Julia Ward Howe achieved in her lifetime, including her work with the Sanitary Commission and social commitments, all else seemed to pale in the light of that one accomplishment, the song, "Battle Hymn of the Republic." She sold that poem to the Atlantic Monthly where she earned $5.00 for her effort.

Here, in the poem "Bailey's Crossroads," we hear from Julia Ward Howe and the inspiration for her work. One can only imagine the depth of feeling that moved Julia Ward Howe as she watched the Union troops with President Abraham Lincoln on that November day in 1861.

While the story of Bailey's Crossroads is important in our Civil War history, I have a personal attachment to this very property. On July 17, 1897 Elvira Finch Moore's son Millard purchased the property for use as a summer home.

Records indicate that the property fell into disrepair in the 1930's and on December 9, 1942 the house burned to the ground. At the time of the fire, it was owned by Millard J. Moore's two daughters, Ardala and Mildred.

It is another tie that binds Elvira Finch Moore and myself not only to our Civil War history, but to the exact house where Abraham Lincoln stood and watched Union General George McLellan review his troops. This of course being the same site where the poet Julia Ward Howe was inspired to write her poem, and where I humbly attempt to honor her with the poem "Bailey's Crossroads."

GRAND REAPING.

SOUTHERN WOMEN FEELING THE EFFECTS OF REBELLION, AND CREATING BREAD RIOTS.

The Bread Riot in Richmond, Virginia on April 2, 1863

Bread or Blood

April 2, 1863

Something very grievous has just happened I must declare
A bread riot it was of such despair
The starving women of Richmond with their babes to feed
Desperate for food I just grieved
And watched as the mob gathered and cried
"tis food we need our babes may die"
We cannot afford the cost of such wares
The Northern blockade we just want our share
Yet what little there is has gone to our men
Left us with nothing again and again
So that today we decided to march and bring
Our desperation oh! It was maddening
Our arms full of bread and flour and meat
Stopped as Jeff Davis heard our grief
And listened with kindness of our plight
Asked us to disperse without a fight
And so the mob did fall away if you must know
But not without food for their babes in tow
And as I held onto my bread so steadfast
For my baby my baby he may not last
This Civil War for the starving of Richmond you see
Has driven us mad, I am on bended knee

The Bread Riot of Richmond, VA
April 2, 1863

In "Bread or Blood" we hear from an unknown woman living in Richmond. She is sharing her story from the day in April 1863 when the women of Richmond were desperate to feed their families. They rose up and rioted on the Confederate Capital.

In the midst of the Civil War, the residents of Richmond were starving to death. In the Confederate Capital, mostly women and children, were suffering from inflationary prices of food due to the Union blockade of Southern ports. This food shortage caused prices to soar.

The lack of supplies was compounded by foraging armies of both Union and Confederate that ravaged farms and crops throughout the South. In many cases, the food was gone long before it could reach the people in the city. Trapped within the city, with fighting all around, the people of Richmond were starving to death.

This desperate situation came to a head on April 2, 1863 as the women of Richmond rose up and looted the city shops crying out "Bread or Blood."

They smashed windows to grab food, flour, meat, and bread; anything they could find to help their families survive. Even the jewelry and millinery shops were looted.

What could have caused the women of the home front to react so violently? Protecting their families, of course. While they suffered from hunger, it was far worse to see their children go hungry.

Finally, Confederate President Jefferson Davis, along with a group of armed guards, pleaded with the women to disperse. He even reached into his pockets throwing money at them declaring, "You say you are hungry and have no money. Here is all I have; it is not much, but take it." 1

From "The Civil War Chronicle," by Matthew J. Gallman:
". . The crowd now rapidly increased, and numbered, I am sure, more than a thousand women and children. It grew and grew until it reached the dignity of a mob—a bread riot. They impressed all the light carts they met, and marched along silently and in order. They marched through Cary Street and Main, visiting the stores of the speculators and emptying them of their contents. Governor Letcher sent the mayor to read the Riot Act, and as this had no effect on the crowd. The city battalion came up. The women fell back with frightened eyes, but did not obey the order to disperse." 2

Eventually, the women dispersed and the riots ended but the event left a grievous mark on Richmond's history.

In the poem "Bread or Blood" we hear from a woman who is desperate to feed her starving child and who rises up to join the mob. She had no choice.

Women caught in the struggle of the Civil War, who might not have done such a thing in better times, stood up that day to fight for themselves and their children.

The war would last for two more bloody years, two more years of suffering, loss, and desperation. It begs the question, what would we have done?

Cathay Williams aka William Cathay

Cathay Williams aka William Cathay

I'll tell you a story about a soldier during Civil War time
A story that I assure you will never leave your mind
For this is not just any soldier you see
It's the story of Cathay Williams; and her yearning to be free
Perhaps you have not heard of her
Her story is buried in time
But she was an American hero
For this and all sublime
She was born in Missouri in eighteen forty-four
The daughter of an enslaved mother
Need I tell you more?
In eighteen sixty-one the Union came
With the start of the Civil War
Laundress, nurse, and cook, she worked all the same
She followed the infantry all over the country
Under General Sheridan, it was said
And witnessed battles of Pea Ridge and Red River
Of this war and all the bloodshed
Although women could not enlist in the Army
For her love of country and freedom she did
Disguised as a man named William
And for three years, so how she hid
Then signed with all-Black regiment in eighteen sixty-eight
To be part of the legendary Buffalo soldiers
Her bravery, it was consummate
Denied disability pension; illness became her foe
This American hero heralded here; of this we hear and know
For although no stone marks her grave; no date of death to see
The first Black woman who fought in the Army; if only to be free

Cathay Williams

(1844-1893)

In this poem we hear from an unknown woman telling the story of Cathay Williams aka William Cathay. She was the first documented Black woman to enlist, and the only documented woman to serve in the United States Army, while disguised as a man during the Indian Wars.1

Cathay was born in Independence, Missouri in 1844 to an enslaved mother and a free father of color. Her childhood was defined by slavery having been born into it, and as a young woman she worked as a house slave.

With the start of the Civil War in 1861, the Union Army occupied Jefferson City, Missouri where young Cathay was enslaved. During the time of the Civil War slaves were considered contraband by the Union or were treated as captured enemy (Confederate) property. With the Union being anti-slavery the recently freed Blacks were given jobs to work in military support of the Union Army as cooks, nurses, and laundresses. The Union would eventually pay wages for their efforts.

At the young age of 17, Cathay served as a Union Army cook and washerwoman. She followed the Army infantry all over the country while under the services of Union General Phillip Sheridan. Despite all odds and defying the prohibition against women serving in the military, Cathay cut her hair and enlisted in the U.S. Regular Army on November 15, 1866 under the name of William Cathay. She continued to serve disguised as a man!

Her gender was eventually revealed on October 14, 1868 during a medical exam and she was given an honorable discharge.

Cathay was still compelled to serve and later went on to enlist with the legendary Buffalo Soldiers, an all-Black regiment after the Civil War.

After many years of service, Cathay suffered from neuralgia and diabetes. She applied for a military disability pension. She was denied. The exact date of her death and burial are unknown although it is assumed it was around 1893, following her denial for a disability pension.

She was a strong and brave Black woman who fought in the United States Army. So incredibly heroic in a tumultuous time, it is here we honor the memory of a woman named Cathay Williams aka William Cathay, whose sacrifice and bravery are steeped in the history of our Civil War.

(Left) Artist William Jennings'
fictional illustration of Cathay Williams

(Right) The monument to Williams located in
Leavenworth, TX by Eddie Dixon

The Garthwright House located in Richmond, Virginia. This was the site of the Union Hospital for the Battle of Cold Harbor, June 1864.

Cold Harbor, Virginia

June 3, 1864

Although I have nursed a thousand or more
Upon the battlefields like ne'er before
And tried my best each and every time
To aid and pray to the one divine
There was a battle of which I could not believe
The death and destruction of soldiers so I grieved
For all the Union men that perished in a flash
Seven thousand it was, burned to ash
My heart was beyond broken, my soul afire
No tears left I had, it was so dire
And doubly so when I spied a young man
Deceased he was, yet I saw in his hand
A diary of some kind held firm in his grasp
Speckled in blood, I was aghast
And knelt to take a look to see
Of whom this soldier ought to be
I opened the diary and saw he was from
A Massachusetts man, God's will was done
I searched for a name, none to be found
And saw the last entry, it was so profound
June 3rd of sixty-four, I read with a chill
Cold Harbor Virginia, I was killed

Battle of Cold Harbor

May 31 - June 12, 1864

The Overland Campaign was conducted by Union General Ulysses S. Grant in the spring of 1864. It would for all intent and purposes be one of the bloodiest and most deadly campaigns for both the Union and the Confederacy. In this poem "Cold Harbor, Virginia" we hear the voice of a woman who was at Cold Harbor, nursing soldiers and witnessed the horrific destruction. The nurse finds the diary of a soldier who lost his life in this battle, a man without a name, yet his final entry predicted his own death.

It was Grant's plan to follow General Robert E. Lee, to destroy the Army of Northern Virginia and preserve the Union. The Overland Campaign began in early May of 1864 at the Battle of the Wilderness where, just one year prior, the Army of Northern Virginia had a tremendous victory over the Union Army of the Potomac at the Battle of Chancellorsville.

At the Battle of Chancellorsville in May 1863, with great odds against victory and by taking chances, General Robert E. Lee along with General Stonewall Jackson would successfully defeat Union General Joseph Hooker. It was a great tactical victory for the Confederacy but came at a greater loss with the death of General Jackson.

May 1864 found Grant and Lee fighting one another for the first time. The Battle of the Wilderness was a draw with no gain for either side, but with appalling losses of men in the thousands. Especially heinous was the 200 Federal soldiers burned alive in the thick and dry underbrush of the Wilderness that caught fire from the heavy musketry and firing of weapons. The Union had 17,000 casualties, the Confederacy 13,000.

It has been said the turning point of the war came right after this battle. After experiencing such a terrible conflict, the Union would have normally retreated. This time they pushed forward and were steadfast to their cause, staying in the constant pursuit of Lee. Heavy fighting continued right up to the Spotsylvania Courthouse.

The loss of men at this battle, again for the Union, totaled over 18,000 and the Confederacy lost 12,000 lives. The fighting would then move to Cold Harbor where in only 20 short minutes more than 7,000 Union soldiers were killed.

General Grant said of this battle, "*I have always regretted that the last assault at Cold Harbor was ever made. I might say the same thing of the assault of the 22nd of May, 1863, at Vicksburg. At Cold Harbor no advantage whatever was gained to compensate for the heavy loss we sustained.*"[1]

Many of the Union soldiers in the failed assault had predicted the outcome, including a dead soldier from Massachusetts whose last entry in his diary was, "*June 3, 1864, Cold Harbor, Virginia. I was killed.*"[2]

During this one month of battles the soldiers were living on the edge of death at every moment. The unknown woman in the poem sees this soldier numbered amongst the dead after the battle and the words in his diary June 3, 1864, Cold Harbor, Virginia, "*I was killed.*"

There is such agony in those words. Imagine writing one's own epitaph on the field of battle, taking the last breath with just enough life to share one's last moment on this earth.

It is heartbreaking, poignant, and unforgettable.

The burning of Columbia, South Carolina on
February 17, 1865 as sketched by W. Waud

Columbia, South Carolina
February 1865

I heard the thunder I heard the roar
It was Sherman's men I begged to implore
Do not burn my house I cried on my knee
There were no slaves here yearning to be free
Just this small patch of earth
Me and my husband Caleb for all it is worth
He done gone now killed up yonder a ways
Cold Harbor it was I beg you please
See here it's just me and my children I cried
The tears were streaming, I had no pride
The children came running out into the night
Watching the soldiers with eyes of fright
The soldiers held their torches high in the air
As we watched and waited in utter despair
God help me please I begged and cried
Without this house we cannot survive
Then like an angel on blessed wings
The Yankee solder did sling
His torch to the ground and ordered the same
To all the Yankees that came
To burn as much they can
Is Columbia, South Carolina where I stand
The Yankee in blue then spoke to me
My children, my children grasping at my knee
Fear not this night from my men here
We will not burn your house do not fear
You see I have a wife and little ones too
The time is now to forgive, to begin anew
He then turned on his heels and ordered his men
Further up the road I prayed for all then
And thought of God's gift that was bestowed on me
I shall never forget, that Yankee, I was blessed you see

Columbia, South Carolina
February 1865

The early months of the year 1865 would bring the Civil War to its conclusion. The end of the war came at the hands of Union General William T. Sherman and his army. He would cut a swath of destruction across the land from the burning of Atlanta, Georgia in the summer of 1864 to his march toward the sea at Savannah, Georgia, in December of 1864.

General Sherman's plan was to take the war directly to the Southern people by destroying property and all that could aid in the Confederacy.

It was when Sherman's great army of 65,000 turned northwards from Georgia toward South Carolina that the burning of its capital city of Columbia took place. Since South Carolina was the first state to secede from the Union on December 20, 1860, General Sherman and his great army held South Carolina in contempt and blamed that state for the start of the Civil War.

Here, his final acts of war were most strongly felt.

General Sherman later publicly claimed that he never ordered the capital city's burning; rather he ordered the artillery not to shell Columbia in order to protect its citizens and property.

The Union Army, in turn, publicly blamed the Confederate officers who ordered bales of cotton in the streets to be burned before retreating from the fire. This is a contradiction to what city resident's recorded, that Union soldiers purposely set fire to the buildings.

Whoever was to blame, Union or Confederacy, the result was the same, South Carolina's capital was ablaze. All citizens including freed slaves, women, and innocent children were caught in the horror of that night.

In this poem, "Columbia, South Carolina, February 1865" we hear from an unknown woman who is begging the Union not to burn her home as the great army stands united before her and her children.

She cries to them, saying she has nowhere to go. Her husband was killed at Cold Harbor, Virginia. She is bereft in her fear and in her plight. At that fateful moment, a Union officer steps forward from the throng of soldiers and they lower their torches. Her home and her children are spared.

Perhaps during the course of the Civil War an act of humanity such as this did transpire. One can only hope. Again, not all Civil War events made it into the history books. It is left to the imagination and having faith in humanity that this woman and her children were spared the destruction of Union General Sherman and his soldiers.

It is most certainly, to hope and to wonder.

Elizabeth Thorn memorial statue located at
Evergreen Cemetery, Gettysburg

Evergreen Cemetery
Gettysburg 1863

It was in July of eighteen sixty-three
An event happened here in Gettysburg you see
A three day battle of North and South
That raged and raged there was no doubt
And the conclusion although the North reigned supreme
Was death and destruction beyond all dreams
My husband although he did fight
For the Union cause it was right
And left me here a caretaker you see
Of Evergreen Cemetery it was to known to be
That after the guns had ceased their fire
Both sides were left ever so dire
I took up my spade and began to bury
The graves of one hundred and five Union, oh so many
My body was heavy with a new life inside
I buried as many as I could
There was no pride
For what I saw in July of sixty-three
Will forever remain within me
I think of those I never knew
Gone now from this earth forever from view
Yet I know in my heart beyond all of this
Almighty God will come and kiss
The faces of those men lost to us on earth
Immortal in God, forever gone forth

Elizabeth Thorn

(1832-1907)
The Angel of Gettysburg

When the Battle of Gettysburg began on July 1, 1863 one local resident named Elizabeth Thorn was working as the caretaker of Evergreen Cemetery, which occupies a hill just south of Gettysburg. This was originally her husband Peter's job, but he was away serving the Union Army with the 138th Pennsylvania and was positioned in Washington D.C. and Harpers Ferry.

Elizabeth was six months pregnant at the time. She lived at the cemetery gatehouse with her three small sons ages seven, five & two, along with her parents.

Due to the strategic location of the cemetery, the Union Major-General Oliver Otis Howard used the gatehouse as his headquarters, lining up artillery brigades along roads on all sides, facing his opponents from every angle.

After three horrifying days of battle, both Evergreen Cemetery and the gatehouse sustained tremendous damage, not only from the thousands of soldiers fighting in hand to hand combat around the area, but from artillery, musket, and canister fire. With nowhere else to go, the Thorn family took refuge in the cellar while war was being waged around them.

Following the battle, outside in the stifling July heat, scores of dead soldiers lay strewn about the hillside and around Gettysburg. This, in conjunction with the horrible screams of the wounded and dying men on the battlefield were the sights and sounds Elizabeth Thorn witnessed.

Her home had been used as a battlefield hospital, with surgery and amputations occurring on her own bed, ruining what few possessions her family had.

Elizabeth later described the scene, *"everything in the house was gone except three feather beds and a couple of pillows. The beds and a dozen pillows we had brought from the old country (Germany) were not fit to use again. The legs of six soldiers had been amputated on the beds in our house and they were ruined with blood and we had to make way with them."* 1

Outside was a horrendous sight, far worse than the damage to her home. The cemetery spanning the hilltop was littered with bodies of dead soldiers with no one to properly bury them. Shouldering her role as caretaker, Elizabeth faced a monumental task. In the three weeks after Gettysburg, this mother of three, who was also far into her pregnancy, buried 105 Union soldiers in the broiling July sun.

In this poem, "Evergreen Cemetery" we hear from Elizabeth telling us the story of that time, not for laurels or plaudits, but to describe her efforts and concerns to provide a proper burial for those brave Union soldiers.

There is a statue created in honor of Elizabeth Thorn at Evergreen Cemetery where she and her husband Peter are buried. The statue depicts Elizabeth with a spade in one hand and wiping her brow with the other, her apron covering her pregnancy. The anguish depicted on the face of Elizabeth is almost palpable.

Elizabeth Thorn has been called the "Angel of Gettysburg" for her heroic efforts in those harrowing days and weeks after the battle. Her statue is formally known as "The Gettysburg Women's Civil War Memorial." It stands beside the Cemetery Gatehouse, where she and Peter lived for 19 years and it represents the work of all the women who were involved in the Civil War.

I believe she rests in heaven with the souls of those Union soldiers, whom she so selflessly gave a proper burial, over 150 years ago upon the battlefield and in a hallowed place, a place called Gettysburg.

The view from behind President Lincoln's chair
at Ford's Theater. Is this what Booth saw?
Author's own photo

Ford's Theater

April 14, 1865

I know I had seen him before
I pondered this as I saw his face
Never thinking that he would become
The cause of such disgrace
It was that night Good Friday
I went to Ford's Theater to see
A lively comedy to lighten the heart,
Or so it seemed to be
Such joy and laughter the war was over I state
April 9th of sixty-five, the South had met their fate
Washington so jubilant, the Union is now as one
We welcomed back our Southern kin, forgiveness has begun
I dressed ever so carefully my beau was at my side
My finest frock for just this night, I felt just like a bride
It was just after ten when I spied the handsome gent
Silently as he went
His fetching face with no smile
Creeping quietly he was, I wondered of his guile
Then in such gaiety as the play did bring
I heard the sound of a shot
We thought it was part of the play
God help us, it was not
Then quick as a cat I saw him leap o'er the balcony
From where our President did sit
Screams then did fill the air
God help us I did admit
Then shrieks and shouts from every corner
Did fill the theater so complete
I now know the handsome man
John Wilkes Booth had sealed his fate

Assassination of
President Abraham Lincoln

Ford's Theater, Washington D.C.
April 14, 1865

It must have been electrifying and yet horrifying all at the same time to be in the audience at Ford's Theater on the evening of April 14, 1865. That day was a Friday that year, Good Friday to be exact. The formal surrender of General Robert E. Lee to General Ulysses S. Grant on April 9, 1865 had signaled the end of the Civil War.

The fighting was over. The suffering and bloodshed had finally ended. Washington was in a state of celebration, only to be violently cut short by an assassin's bullet.

The history of the assassination of President Abraham Lincoln on April 14, 1865 at Ford's Theater by southern sympathizer and actor, John Wilkes Booth, is a night that never ceases to lose its grievous impact even though it occurred over 150 years ago.

President Lincoln loved the theater; he attended over 100 performances during his presidency. It was no surprise then on the morning of April 14, 1865 that Ford's Theater would be advised that President and Mrs. Lincoln would be present at that night's performance, "Our American Cousin."

They intended to be accompanied by General Ulysses S. Grant and his wife Julia. However, due to previous disagreements between Julia Grant and Mrs. Lincoln, the Grants decided to make other plans that evening, traveling instead to visit their children in New Jersey.

The Lincoln's would then ask Major Henry Rathbone and his fiancée Clara Harris to join them. She was the daughter of President Lincoln's good friend, New York Senator, Ira Harris.

The presidential party arrived late to the theater that night. The play had already begun. The cast stopped performing as the orchestra played "Hail to the Chief" to honor the President while those 1,700 people in attendance gave him a standing ovation, after which the play resumed.

View of the Presidential Box at Ford's Theater
Author's own photo

Earlier that day the well-known actor John Wilkes Booth had stopped at Ford's Theater to pick up his mail when he learned that the President, Mrs. Lincoln, along with General and Mrs. Grant would be attending that evening.

In addition to being an actor, John Wilkes Booth was an ardent southern sympathizer and a blockade runner for the Confederacy.

He did not enlist in the Confederacy to fight due to a promise made to this mother. He became increasingly agitated about this fact. In his own self-loathing he considered himself a coward for not enlisting.

He believed Lincoln was a tyrant.

After the fall of Richmond on April 3, 1865, which was the Capital of the Confederacy after which followed the surrender of General Robert E. Lee to General Ulysses S. Grant on April 9, 1865 at Appomattox Courthouse, Booth became more agitated. He eventually made the fateful decision to assassinate President Lincoln. He believed by doing so it would give the South the opportunity to rise again.

John Wilkes Booth was familiar with Ford's Theater. He had acted there on several occasions and he knew the play "Our American Cousin" very well. He performed it many times as a stock actor at the Richmond Theater (1858-1860). That knowledge gave him opportunity to not only enter the theater without being questioned, but also the timing to approach the President at an opportune moment.

As the play reached a point of comedy, where he knew the audience would be noisily laughing, Booth crept along the wall on the second floor of Ford's Theater and made his way toward the Presidential Box.

There he shot President Lincoln in the back of the head, then fought and slashed Major Rathbone with his knife. Booth leapt over the balcony, but in his jump to escape, his spur caught on the decorative bunting of the Presidential Box and he landed awkwardly on the stage, breaking his left leg.

John Wilkes Booth rose up holding the bloody knife in his hand and cried out "Sic Semper Tyrannis", which means "thus always to tyrants," Virginia's state motto which is depicted on the state flag.

President Lincoln would die the next morning at 7:22 am from his terrible head wound. He was in the back bedroom of the Petersen House across the street from Ford's Theater where he was taken after the assassination.

Booth would be on the run for 12 days. He would die on April 26, 1865 from a gunshot wound in the back of the neck, fired by the Union New York Calvary. He was hiding at the Garrett Farm in Port Royal, Virginia.

In this poem, "Ford's Theater" we hear from an unknown woman who was in the audience that fateful night. She is enjoying the play "Our American Cousin," yet during the performance she notices John Wilkes Booth silently creeping towards President Lincoln's Box. She hears the shot and witnesses Booth jumping over the balcony onto the stage.

A moment never to be forgotten. A moment frozen in time. A moment frozen in history.

I have visited Ford's Theater many times and viewed the Presidential Box up close. Seeing the stage below and knowing what happened there so many years ago reminded me of the agony of that loss. A loss that still resonates with us today.

Steps and trail leading up to Big Round Top
Gettysburg National Military Park
Author's own photo

Have You Seen My Caleb?

Colonel Chamberlain, can you help my heart?
My darling Caleb he did part
And joined the 20th Maine under your command
To protect the Union and the task at hand
When last I did hear from my beloved you see
Marching to Gettysburg it was to be
Forces of men and guns
So much death God's will was done
Of your valor upon Little Round Top it was called
Where the 20th of Maine stood tall and proud
And proved themselves at your dare
To repel the Rebels beyond compare
For you see Colonel Chamberlain
I must know now
Of where my Caleb is I do avow
For a mourning dove did greet me this morn
Upon my windowsill, I am so forlorn
And heard the cries of this tiny dove
A message I know from God above
Find my Caleb, dear Colonel I implore
And tell him his wife does adore
All that he is and ever will be
Colonel Chamberlain, can you help me?

Joshua Lawrence Chamberlain

(1828-1914)

When the Civil War began in April 1861, Joshua Lawrence Chamberlain, who was born Lawrence Joshua Chamberlain, was a professor at Bowdoin College in Maine teaching rhetoric and modern languages. He had a strong desire to fight for the Union and asked for a leave of absence. However, many of the professors at the college felt differently and his request for a leave to serve in the military was denied.

In 1862 he applied for a sabbatical to study languages in Europe. It was granted and Chamberlain promptly enlisted in the 20th Maine Voluntary Infantry. There he was given the rank of Lieutenant Colonel.

He would rise to become a highly respected officer in the Union Army. July 2, 1863 would find Colonel Chamberlain and his regiment holding the extreme left position of the Union lines located at Little Round Top at the Battle of Gettysburg.

Chamberlain's men withstood multiple assaults by the Confederate 15th Alabama Infantry. He conducted what was considered a textbook military maneuver, this coming from a college professor. With little ammunition left for his soldiers, Colonel Chamberlain enacted a bayonet charge down Little Round Top, surprising the advancing Confederates and overwhelming them.

The charge saved the day's battle and perhaps even the war itself. For his superior leadership at Little Round Top, Colonel Chamberlain was awarded the Medal of Honor.

He also participated in several other prominent battles in the war. He would later sustain what was thought to be a mortal wound at the Second Battle of Petersburg in 1864. Yet he miraculously survived and was promoted on the field at

Petersburg to Brigadier General. He was also present at the surrender of Confederate General Robert E. Lee's Army at Appomattox Court House, Virginia April 9, 1865.

The story of Joshua Lawrence Chamberlain and his famous bayonet charge at Little Round Top on July 2, 1863 is considered the turning point for the North at the Battle of Gettysburg.

The poem, "Have You Seen My Caleb?" introduces another aspect of war. In it we hear the heartbreaking echoes of an unknown woman who is reaching out for word of her husband.

I have hiked up both Little Round Top and Big Round Top at Gettysburg National Military Park. The climb up the hill to Big Round Top was rocky, steep, and difficult. Yet soldiers fought on this ground. It was while standing at the summit on both these locations that the enormity of what happened there resonated within me.

It was as if the voice of this unknown woman swept across the Round Tops in agonizing waves of grief.

This is a reminder of the plight of the women of the Civil War, for both North and South, who were left waiting for a letter from a husband, son, father or brother that they had survived the battle. Sadly, for so many women, it is one that never came.

THEY BROUGHT IN THEIR DEAD AND WOUNDED ON HAY WAGONS

Photo from the Library of Richmond, Virginia
as printed in the Civil War Research Guide

In Thine Eyes

In thine eyes my most beautiful wife
I saw perfection that gave me life
And stopped my heart at my very first glance
Eyes of violet I took a chance
The eyes beholden that bended my knee
That took my breath and all of me
To such beauty I have never seen
A gift from the Almighty that reigns supreme
And so I think upon your eyes
As I sit before the battle, we will rise
And soon dear wife it will come again
The charge, the fire the loss of men
I must tell you my darling my wife and admit
Tis not long for this earth I must submit
For the angel of death has come for me
My wounds to grave, never to be
But know dear wife as I write to you
I see thine eyes violet in hue
And as I lose my eyes to the sight
The last of earth will all my might
And as I ascend with the Almighty at my side
Wait for me dear wife, so now I cry

Violet in Hue

Here we have a love poem, for love is often the only good we have left to hold onto in the midst of war.

This particular poem, "In Thine Eyes" is from an unknown soldier, neither North or South is indicated, and no battle is referenced. What lies in a man's heart is timeless. This poem simply and heartbreakingly conveys pure love from a husband who is longing to see the beautiful violet eyes of his wife just once more before dying.

It was written for all those unknown soldiers who died without seeing their loved ones one last time. It is also equally written for those unknown wives or girlfriends waiting at home to hear from their brave soldier.

To think of all those hundreds and thousands of soldiers who never came home! It breaks the heart. One can only imagine their last moment on earth was perhaps spent thinking of their wife's beautiful eyes, as they closed their own in death.

Excerpt from a famous love letter
by Union officer Sullivan Ballou
to his wife Sarah.

Headquarters, Camp Clark
Washington, D.C., July 14, 1861

My Very Dear Wife:

....Sarah, my love for you is deathless. It seems to bind me with mighty cables, that nothing but Omnipotence can break; and yet, my love of country comes over me like a strong wind, and bears me irresistibly on with all those chains, to the battlefield. The memories of all the blissful moments I have spent with you

come crowding over me, and I feel most deeply grateful to God and you, that I have enjoyed them so long. And how hard it is for me to give them up, and burn to ashes the hopes of future years, when, God willing, we might still have lived and loved together, and seen our boys grow up to honorable manhood around us.

I know I have but few claims upon Divine Providence, but something whispers to me, perhaps it is the wafted prayer of my little Edgar, that I shall return to my loved ones unharmed. If I do not, my dear Sarah, never forget how much I love you, nor that, when my last breath escapes me on the battle-field, it will whisper your name.1

Major Sullivan Ballou

The only known photo of Janie Wellford Corbin

Confederate General Thomas Stonewall Jackson

Janie Corbin

There is a child I will tell you of the tale that is true
Her name was Janie met her Christmas of sixty-two
'Twas when I made my camp in the winter of that year
Moss Neck Plantation, the Rappahannock was near
And such was the time I spent at her parent's home
The child Janie and I befriended forever known
Lively, endearing that warmed my being
My daughter just born, yet not seeing
And here comes Janie and calls my name
She laughs and giggles all the same
For this lovely child that God has brought forth
Has eased my longing heart for all that its' worth
And now the time has come to bid adieu
For the calling of war rings anew
I bade farewell to the child, I could not ignore
Oh this little girl so how I adore
And so I heard the most distressing of news
Janie had scarlet fever oh I was so blue
But her parents said she would recover just fine
And be well to see the spring so sublime
I breathed a sigh of relief you know
And one day later, please God it is to forego
That my little Janie with the heart of gold
Succumbed to the fever I cannot hold
Her, until such time as God calls me home
Wait for me Janie, we will share the throne

Janie Corbin

(1857-1863)
&

Stonewall Jackson

(1824-1863)

There are stories and events of the Civil War that seem to go beyond the realm of heartbreak. The story of Janie Corbin and Confederate General Thomas J. Stonewall Jackson is just such one of them.

While in camp in the winter of 1862-1863, General Jackson resided at Moss Neck Plantation, outside Fredericksburg, Virginia. The owners of the residence had several children; the youngest was Janie at five years old. A friendship and love grew between Janie and General Jackson.

He adored Janie, perhaps thinking of his own daughter Julia, who was born November 22, 1862 and whom he would not see until April 1863 when she was five months old. In her book, "Memoirs of Stonewall Jackson by His Widow," his wife Anna (Mrs. Jackson) describes the poignant moment when General Jackson first held his own daughter:

"It was raining and he was afraid to take her in his arms with his wet overcoat, but upon arrival at the house, he speedily divested himself of his overcoat, and, taking his baby in his arms, he caressed her with the tenderest affection, and held her long and lovingly. During the whole of this short visit, when he was with us, he rarely had her out of his arms, waking her, and amusing her in every way that he could think of - sometimes holding her up before a mirror and saying, admiringly, "Now, Miss Jackson, look at yourself." Then he would turn to an old lady

*of the family and say, "Isn't she a little gem?" When she slept in the day, he would often kneel over her cradle, and gaze upon her little face with the most rapt admiration, and he said he felt almost as if she were an angel in her innocence and purity."*1

In March 1863, General Jackson left Moss Neck Plantation to prepare camp for spring offensives. While saying goodbye, the General was told Janie had scarlet fever, but would recover. He felt hopeful, assured she would be fine.

Unfortunately, Janie would die within weeks and upon hearing the news, the General was bereft at her passing. The agony of the loss of the little girl was openly displayed by the usually stoic and staunch General Jackson. In this poem, "Janie Corbin" we hear from Jackson himself describing the child and his grief.

Although we know who is speaking in this poem and we know it is about the child Janie, the story reflects the kind of love that is universal between a father and his child. Although she was not his child, their bond was deep. His love for Janie was just too heartbreaking and yet also too poignant not to add to this collection.

Stonewall Jackson would be wounded at the Battle of Chancellorsville on May 2, 1863. He would succumb to death from pneumonia on May 10. His wife Anna and baby daughter Julia were by his side at the time of his death.

His last words were, *"Let us cross over the river and rest under the shade of the tree."*2 One cannot help but wonder, if in fact the child Janie was there in heaven resting under the shade of that tree, waiting for him.

Jack Skelly

Jennie Wade

Jennie & Jack

There are some stories in those Civil War times
That do not fade from the heart
Of anguish and grief and loss you see
To this is how I start
On July 3, of eighteen sixty-three the Battle of Gettysburg raged
Upon the dwelling of Jennie and kin
Caught in the fire of North and South
Caught in the battle din
Yet this house was set in between
The shots fire and explode about
Grateful you see they would be alright
Of this they had no doubt
But it was an unfortunate fire
From the Farnworth's house set up just a ways
That found its way into the sweet Jennie
Kneading bread that day
Within an instant her life was gone you see
Not even a moment to cry
Her life and blood ebbed free upon the floor
Not our Jennie to die!
Yet there is more thing to state of this very sad tale
One that brings tears to the eye
For Jennie's beau would soon also pass
Of this I cannot lie
And so they passed; each one not knowing of their fate
A sad story yes it is; yet there one more thing to state
For in the photo you see the lovely Jennie's face
Yet no reflection of her is seen
But rather the face of her darling Jack
Together at last it seems
For what was taken in death you see
Cannot forever be gone
For two lovers lost in life
In death they are yet reborn

Jennie Wade
(1843-1863)
&
Jack Skelly
(1841-1863)

One of the Civil War's most tragic stories of innocent lives being caught up in the destruction of war is that of Jennie Wade. She was in fact the only civilian to be killed during the three day Battle of Gettysburg. Jennie, her mother, and her brother had fled the oncoming battle to take safe refuge inside the home of her sister, Georgia McClellan.

Jennie wanted to help the Union. The women were baking bread for the Union Army in the kitchen on the morning of July 3, 1863. They believed they were safe inside. But suddenly a stray bullet found its way through the kitchen door and into Jennie. It was believed the shot came from a Confederate sharpshooter. She died instantly. She was just 20 years old.

To further the heartache of this incredible tragic story is what occurred with Jennie's fiancé, Jack Skelly, a Union corporal serving in the 87th Pennsylvania. He had been wounded a few weeks earlier at the Battle of Winchester. Jack would later die of his wounds on July 12.

This story becomes even more heartbreaking when the childhood friend of both Jennie and Jack, a Confederate private named Wesley Culp, would find his friend Jack in a field hospital. Jack asked Wesley to deliver a note to his fiancée Jennie. As with so many stories of the Civil War this one ends in bonds of sorrow. Unfortunately, Wesley was killed on July 3, the same day as Jennie, and his death occurred on property that was owned by his family, Culp's Hill.

Jennie would never receive the note, nor would she or Jack know of each other's death. They are however buried beside one another in Evergreen Cemetery, Gettysburg.

I had an incredible opportunity to visit the Jennie Wade House and walk the same floors as Jennie did, all those years ago. I could almost feel the family's grief of the passing of this innocent young woman. The sense of loss hangs over this house, especially in the kitchen where the stray bullet crashed through the door and into Jennie.

Directly off the kitchen is the bedroom where Jennie's sister Georgia had given birth to a baby boy just days before the battle. There is a bullet lodged in the top left bedpost, as well as multiple bullet holes that are visible throughout the house.

The exterior door of the kitchen of the Jennie Wade House
Note: the bullet hole in the door still visible today.
Author's own photo

However, it is the photo of Jennie that is hanging over the mantle and the reflection it casts into the mirror above the bed that caught my attention.

For if you look closely at the reflected image in the mirror it bears a striking resemblance to Jennie's fiancé Jack.

Fact or fiction?

This is the 1st floor bedroom of The Jennie Wade House in Gettysburg. Note the reflection in the mirror above the bed where Jennie's portrait resembles Jack Skelly in an almost haunting display.
Author's own photo

Perhaps this is Jack finding a way to stay close to Jennie beyond the grave. Theirs is a heartbreaking story. It is of a brave young woman who had her dreams and future with her fiancé Jack stolen by the Civil War. She was cut down before her life really had a chance to begin.

As in this case, sometimes the passing of time does nothing to ease the profound sadness of this true story. It is my belief that perhaps there are things we cannot explain and some Civil War stories too grievous and heartbreaking to fathom. This most certainly is one of them.

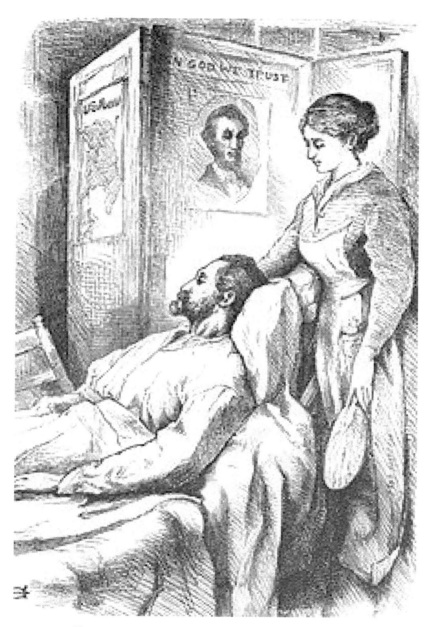

Illustration of John, a Virginia blacksmith
from a later edition of "Hospital Sketches"
by Louisa May Alcott

John, A Virginia Blacksmith

I awoke from a fitful slumber and took a look around
I am in hospital not sure where to be found
And took some time to try to see
A kindly nurse set before me
I said to her with the utmost care
My name is John from Virginia is where
I used to blacksmith for my family's fare
My ma and little sisters I have to bear
You see, I put off marriage for some time
As my ma had no one left to be kind
And so with the war I did enlist
To protect my family from the invaders at risk
I had to go to protect them you see
And now I sit with minie ball in me
So I dared asked her name and with the kindest of smile
Said Louise May Alcott, I'll sit for a while
She reached for my hand with tears I could see
A gesture I feared was the end of me
I done took off my ring it was my Ma's you know
And gave it to Miss Alcott to have and to hold
And asked her kindly as it pained my heart
To send it to my Ma, it was time to part

Louisa May Alcott

(1832-1888)

Louisa May Alcott, the author of the famous American novel, "Little Women" also volunteered in the Civil War as a Union nurse in 1862. She left her family's home in Concord, Massachusetts to work at the war hospitals in Washington D.C. for six months.

Unfortunately, while nursing the soldiers, she contracted typhoid fever which would end her nursing career and adversely affected her heath for the rest of her life. She was sent back to Massachusetts to convalesce. However, during her time in the Washington D.C. hospitals, Louisa would pen six letters or "sketches" that detailed her nursing experience to her family.

These letters would later be published in 1863 by a company in Boston, Massachusetts, as a lightly fictionalized book called "Hospital Sketches."

There is one timeless sketch that is truly poignant and unforgettable.

Louisa described this one soldier named John, a Virginia blacksmith whom she was nursing. The two had become friends. She was told by the doctors at the hospital that John was dying from a bullet lodged in his lung and although he lingered in life and he believed he would recover; the wound would eventually prove fatal. They could not operate. His death proved to be slow and painful.

Yet somehow this man who was physically suffering so deeply, still had within him the capacity to show warmth and a noble character. Louisa sat with him to ease his pain. She describes how John followed her about with his eyes, his hand reaching out to gently touch her gown as if to reassure himself that she was there.

The doctors couldn't bring themselves to tell John the severity of his wounds. They asked Louisa to do it. She would come to tell John that his wound was fatal and that he would not survive. From that moment forward she stayed at his side.

In his last moments of life, Louisa held his hands, not letting go even after the angel of death had come for John.

It was only after she was told it was unsafe for the living to be so long entwined with the dead that she released his hands, noticing only then the four white marks across the back of her hands from John's fingers.

After he passed away Miss Alcott wrote:

"It was John's letter, come just an hour too late to gladden the eyes that had longed and looked for it so eagerly! yet he had it; for, after I had cut some brown locks for his mother, and taken off the ring to send her, telling how well the talisman had done its work, I kissed this good son for her sake, and laid the letter in his hand, still folded as when I drew my own away, feeling that its place was there, and making myself happy with the thought, that, even in his solitary place in the "Government Lot," he would not be without some token of the love which makes life beautiful and outlives death."[1]

In our poem, "John, A Virginia Blacksmith" we hear John describing Louisa's gentle care of him. It is to wonder that she would have found herself with him in his last moments on this earth watching and caring for him as he unselfishly bore the pain of death.

The experience of this one dying soldier left a mark on Louisa and changed the depth of her writing. She believed that the greatest moments of mankind should be spent in lifting the burden of another, in sharing their suffering to ease their pain. This was an exceptional example of the humanity of history in our Civil War.

Union Drummer Boy

Lorena

Dearest wife I now sit and write
On this eve of battle is time to fight
Here in Atlanta with Sherman we came
July of sixty-four, I do refrain
Yet in the eve of this battle
That will surely create—death-destruction it is our fate
I heard a tune that seemed to drift
Across the battle lines I must admit
And such was the sound from the cornet I believe
That song that halted me I could not breathe
It was Lorena I heard played in a mournful tune
The words and memory of which I did croon
And dear wife you would not believe
What happened next I do not deceive
But for that moment when the song was played
Both North and South did halt their dismay
And forgot in that moment that we were of North
But rather bound together in the beauty brought forth
And as the melody faded to night
The call to arms it was our plight
But for a moment we all knew
The melody of Lorena, dear wife—adieu

Lorena

Lorena was a popular love ballad during the Civil War. It was embraced and played by both the North and the South. The sad story behind the song, which was composed and written by Henry Webster in 1857 was that the ballad was written after his fiancée ended their engagement.

During the Civil War, the song struck a chord in people's hearts and became a woeful representation of the separation of loved ones both North and South. It evoked such emotion and feelings of separation and homesickness that, according to folklore, it aided in the desertion of soldiers after hearing it.

Legend also says that in some instances generals and officers forbade the song from even being played in camp. One Confederate officer even attributed the South's defeat to the song. He reasoned that upon hearing the mournful ballad the soldiers grew so homesick that they lost their effectiveness as a fighting force.

The second stanza is particularly heart wrenching:

"A hundred months have passed, Lorena,
Since last I held thy hand in mine;
And felt the pulse beat fast, Lorena,
Though mine beat faster far than thine;
A hundred months,'twas flowery May,
When up the hilly slope we climbed,
To watch the dying of the day,
And hear the distant church bells chime."

However, Lorena's popularity is not just limited to the 19th century and the Civil War. Lorena appears in the 20th century as well. The haunting, woeful melody has a place in a 1956 film directed by John Ford called "The Searchers" starring John Wayne.

"The musical score for "The Searchers" was written by Max Steiner. The soundtrack includes the music just as it was utilized in various scenes within the film. A portion of the antebellum tune, 'Lorena', is incorporated, without lyrics, into the following scenes: "Ethan Returns" (1:49); "Goodbye Ethan" (0:44); and, the "End Title" (2:12); which fades into the Sons of the Pioneers singing "Ride Away". However, Steiner never utilized "Lorena" in its entirety anywhere in the musical score."[1]

Then in the fall of 1990 the full tune of Lorena was played throughout the Ken Burns PBS documentary series, "The Civil War." The melody is heard in various segments throughout the documentary woven in such a way that it resonates and pulls at the very heartstrings with each touching segment.

In this poem, "Lorena" an unknown solider from the Union is at the Battle of Atlanta. He is writing to his wife telling her how every evening at dusk a Confederate sharpshooter from Georgia would rise and play the melancholy tune of Lorena with his cornet. The touching strains of the melody made his heart long for his loved ones at home. The third stanza sums up the depth of that longing:

"We loved each other then, Lorena.
More than we ever dared to tell;
And what we might have been, Lorena,
Had but our lovings prospered well.
But then,'tis past, the years are gone,
I'll not call up their shadowy forms;
I'll say to them, "lost years, sleep on!
Sleep on! Nor heed life's pelting storms." [2]

The beauty of Lorena has spanned the 19th century and then into the 20th century. Listen just once and you will forever remember the haunting refrain of the woeful lamenting tune.

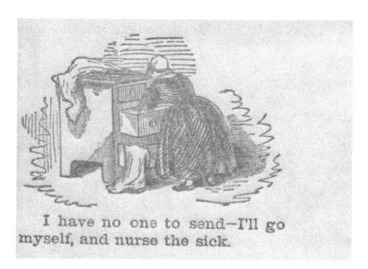

I have no one to send—I'll go myself, and nurse the sick.

Civil War Era envelope depicting Mother Bickerdyke from The New York Historical Society/Getty Images

Mary Ann "Mother" Bickerdyke

Mother Bickerdyke

In the Civil War years of sixty-one to sixty-five
Through battle after battle, never thought to survive
Our Union men in need of such care
Crying out for help in oh such despair
That an angel of mercy did appear early on
To aid our soldiers whose agony was upon
And followed through the fields that kill
Brave and selfless through heat and chill
She tended us with gentle grace
Cooking, nursing and never in haste
For each soldier she gave the utmost care
For such a woman is so very rare
That indeed I bolded to ask her name
"Mother" Bickerdyke she replied, or so I became
It was aid and care she gave for our brave souls
To fight for freedom for those unknowns
And cleanse the earth of the taskmaster's ways
And free a nation, a nation of slaves
So then I heard a most incredible boast
That shouted out like a heavenly host
"She ranks me," I heard him speak
It was General Sherman who came to seek
Of her greatest gift to us Union men
Our "Mother" Bickerdyke, again and again

Mary Ann "Mother" Bickerdyke

(1817-1901)

Mary Ann "Mother" Bickerdyke was a woman who had a deep commitment and compassion for the Union soldiers. She attended Oberlin College in Cincinnati, Ohio, one of the few institutions of higher learning that were open to women at that time. In 1847 she married Robert Bickerdyke and they moved to Galesburg, Illinois where they had two sons.

Unfortunately, in 1859 her husband Robert died, leaving her the sole supporter of the family. She worked as a domestic and a nurse to support them.

Feeling her call to duty when the Civil War began, she sent supplies and began nursing at the Cairo, Illinois hospital. It was there she met Union General Ulysses S. Grant. General Grant was observant of her compassionate efforts to treat the wounded soldiers and developed a trust in her. He would then see to it that she received passes to be in the Union camps.

She followed General Grant and the army to Corinth and Vicksburg, Mississippi and many other battles and battlefields during the Civil War. Her determination and steadfast devotion to the soldiers was unswerving. She would commonly risk her own life in the course of a battle while out searching for wounded soldiers on the battlefield. When night fell, she would take a lantern searching between the battle lines, at great risk to herself, to retrieve the wounded.

She was in fact also held in high favor with Union General William T. Sherman, so much so he said of her "she ranks me."[1] She was of the highest regard in the tending of her soldiers. After the war she provided legal assistance to help those soldiers who needed legal aid, as well in assisting over 300 women nurses in securing their pensions.

It was written of "Mother" Bickerdyke:

"While some of the nurses in the Civil War were organized by religious orders or under Dorothea Dix's command, Mary Ann Bickerdyke represents another kind of nurse: a volunteer who was not responsible to any supervisor, and who often interjected themselves into camps where women were forbidden to go."[2]

Mary Ann "Mother" Bickerdyke brought hope, determination, and compassion to the Union soldiers during the Civil War. It was said that General Sherman regarded her as a General. Soldiers viewed her as a mother. History reveres her as a heroine of the highest caliber.

She was most certainly all of these, but it was her selflessness and duty to those long ago brave soldiers that was truly her greatest achievement.

Mary Ann Holmes Booth

My Absalom

I remember at the time of your birth
Mother's favored of all her boys
There came to her a premonition
That cut her soul from joy
For in the firelight
Of when she nested you tight
She saw the flames rise and fall
And told me of your plight
I knew then as the flames danced and licked
The crackling wood within
That somehow some way my brother
There would no absolution from sin
And as I watched you grow and change
Into the handsomest man of all
Yet in your heart raged some hate
Of this it would befall
Such fame you had notwithstanding
A mother's love as I knew
To save you from impending doom
For this I bid adieu
Yet do we know the story of Absalom?
King's David's third most boy
Like you my darling Johnny
Created in such to destroy
So what of a mother's love
Who cried for you on her knee
A life so misunderstood
My darling my Absalom, you are now free

John Wilkes Booth

(1838-1865)

John Wilkes Booth was born on May 10, 1838 in Bel Air, Maryland in a log cabin home on the family farm. He was the ninth of ten children born to Mary Ann Holmes Booth and Junius Brutus Booth the well-known actor. John was the favored child of both parents. Mary Ann said, "*John was the most pleasure and comfort to me of all my sons, the most affectionate.*"1 When he grew up he said, he would take the greatest care to see that she was happy.

When John was about six months old Mary Ann had a strong premonition that he would die an early and unnatural death. This fateful image stayed with her and with his sister Asia.

John Wilkes Booth was close to his sister Asia Booth Clarke. In the aftermath of his assassination of President Lincoln, she wrote "John Wilkes Booth, A Sister's Memoir" which was completed in 1874, mostly from memory. This secret memoir was hidden from her husband John Sleeper Clark as he blamed the Booth family, especially John Wilkes, for his problems. Asia died in 1888, but prior to her death she gave the book to the family to be published. Unfortunately, it would not be published until 1938, fifty years later. This is the longest and most extensive account by a family member of John Wilkes Booth.

Through Asia a picture of John's life from his childhood up to his tragic death is poignantly brought forth. She provides insights and emotional reminiscences of their time together growing up at Tudor Hall in Bel Air, Maryland in the mid 1850's. Living in the relative isolation of the Maryland countryside, the two were constant companions. Close in age, they shared their love of poetry and music. Long talks on the porch or before the fire filled the evening hours. Here they were "lonely together,"2 as Asia expressed it.

As the Booth family writer and chronicler, Asia wrote two more books giving insight into the pain her family endured after John assassinated President Lincoln. Published in 1866, one book is called, "Booth Memorials. Passages, Incidents and Anecdotes in the life of Junius Brutus Booth (the elder)."

Here she cries out, *"calamity, without precedent has fallen on our country! We, of all families, secure in domestic love and retirement, are stricken desolate! The name we would have enwreathed in laurels is dishonored by a son, -his well-beloved-his bright boy Absalom!"*3

Asia is referencing the Biblical story of Absalom from King David's third son. John Wilkes was the third Booth son as well. The Bible says Absalom was praised as the most handsome man in all Israel: *"He was flawless from head to foot." (2 Samuel 14:25, NLT) When he cut his hair once a year—only because it became too heavy—it weighed five pounds. It seemed everyone loved him."*4 John was also praised as being the handsomest man in America. Absalom revolted against his own father and tried to steal his kingdom, whereupon he was not successful and destroyed himself. Similarly, John Wilkes was shot to death on April 26, 1865 in Port Royal, Virginia after being hunted by the Union Army for the assassination of President Lincoln.

In "My Absalom" we hear from Asia reflecting on John, who loved his mother, was incredibly famous and handsome, yet the fire that raged within him ultimately drove him to destruction. She mentions the vision Mary Ann saw in the firelight when John was just a baby, it spelled out "Country" and that John would die an early and unnatural death.

How grievous for Mary Ann when her vision came true! Asia's comparison between King David's favored son Absalom and her brother John is very apt, indeed.

Her lament and comparison to her brother John calls out from her broken heart through the disgraced name of the third son of King David, his well-beloved-his bright boy Absalom. This comes from her third book, "Booth Memorials" and it is the second paragraph in her Introduction. Placed there on purpose, not to be missed, stating unequivocally the author's pain.

John Wilkes Booth, unknown photographer

Asia Booth Clarke in the 1850's

My Brother Johnny

I called your name into the night
Hoping you would come into my sight
For the dream or nightmare I should state
Was of you running towards a destined fate
I see you dear brother in the quiet of my heart
Our youth together perfect as not to part
Remember those sweet hot summer days
Galloping on Cola and never afraid
Or sprouting Shakespeare on your balcony to the east
Welcoming mornings we thought would never cease
And how handsome you were and most favored of all
Charming, delightful without a flaw
Yet thoughts of you were of our most happiest of times
Our youth and care now gone and sublime
By one grievous act you did so commit
And leave me without hope I must now admit
I have tried not see the end that came your way
Hunted by humanity in this you did betray
And shot through the neck and suffered and died
My dear sweet Johnny, forever I cry

John Wilkes Booth

(1838-1865)
&
Asia Booth Clarke

(1835-1888)

History tells us that John Wilkes Booth assassinated Abraham Lincoln, the 16th President of the United States, at Ford's Theater in Washington D.C. on April 14, 1865. The words killer, murderer, and assassin will be forever associated with John Wilkes Booth, and rightfully so.

What we do know about John, his upbringing, his passion for acting and his relationships with his family comes from the written words of his older and closest sister Asia Booth Clarke from her book, "John Wilkes Booth, A Sister's Memoir." In her memoir, a picture of John is poignantly brought to light.

John and Asia were remarkably close growing up together, especially during childhood and their early teen years at the family farm Tudor Hall in Bel Air, Maryland. They also shared fond memories of living in a city townhouse dwelling on North Exeter Street, Baltimore, Maryland.

Although they were destined for different things in life, they remained close even as their lives moved towards the future and into early adulthood. John pursued the dramatic family vocation of acting and thrived, while Asia became a wife and mother, as Asia Booth Clarke.

The love of brother and sister are to be found within the Memoir pages, and the agony Asia felt over his most grievous act is there as well. This still resonates to the reader, over 150 years after John's own murderous end.

It is to Asia we look and find the extraordinary phrase she uses to end her memoir, with a line from Shakespeare's Hamlet "so runs the world away."

From Hamlet Act 3, scene 2 *"for some must watch while some must sleep, so runs the world away."*[1]

These words gave me pause to try to decipher what Asia meant by "so runs the world away" and why she chose this particular line to end her memoir of John. Of all the lines in Shakespeare and all the tragedies, she uses this one. Why is that? What is she trying to tell us?

It is my opinion that it is not so much that John Wilkes Booth performed in so many Shakespearean tragedies, it's perhaps that Asia is saying to us, that in the end not only did John create the greatest of all American tragedies; he in fact became an American tragedy himself.

This haunting refrain from Asia "so runs the world away," is a poignant glimpse into a sister's grief, who is now reunited with her brother, together forever, in oblivion.

Gravestone at the National Cemetery in
Gettysburg National Military Park.
Author's own photo

My Henry

I walked past the patch of earth
That housed my Henry now gone
Silenced forever from my sight
God help me I am so forlorn
Is Gettysburg I tell you now
Whose battle he so valiantly did fight
For our Union he did say
I still love him with all my might
'Tis November now five months has passed since then
So now our President is here, to dedicate our fallen men
And so I heard his words quite beautiful I do say
Like poetry from God above, I bowed my head to pray
It took him just two minutes or so
As the words flowed ever so divine
Like manna from heaven that touched the soul
I know that they did mine
Yet as much as I tried to be near him
The crowd in between too great
I wanted to tell our President, of my Henry's fate
I had to try to reach him to tell him of my heart
It was the look in his eyes that have haunted me
Careworn that gave me a start
For in those eyes it seems he too knew of his fate
And would come to rest I am sure, in the glory of heaven's gate

The Gettysburg Address

November 19, 1863

    The unknown woman in this poem has heard the news that President Lincoln is coming to Gettysburg to dedicate the new National Cemetery for the Union Civil War dead.

    The Battle of Gettysburg occurred just five months earlier on July 1-3, 1863 and this woman's husband Henry was one of the thousands of men who died during the battle. She is still suffering greatly over his loss, yet she resolves to come to the cemetery to hear President Lincoln speak.

    What she hears in the two-minute address is riveting "like poetry from God, I bowed my head to pray."

    She tries to move through the crowd to see him and to tell him about her Henry. The crowd is too much for her to get through, then in an instance he raises his head, and their eyes meet.

    The woman says she foresees Lincoln's own death in his eyes and that the dear President as well knows of his fate. It binds them together for this one fateful moment in time. Yet such comfort she did take away from the President in his brief speech, just 272 words, that would describe his compassion and resolution in faith, the words that defined what was happening to his people.

    President Lincoln would indeed meet his death at the hands of Southern sympathizer, actor, and assassin, John Wilkes Booth at Ford's Theater in Washington D.C. on April 14, 1865. He would in fact end up sacrificing his own life for the freedom and liberty of all his people.

On November 19, 1863 on a platform erected in neighboring Evergreen Cemetery in Gettysburg, President Lincoln said in his address to the people there:

"The world will little note, nor long remember what we say here, but it can never forget what they did here. It is for us the living, rather, to be dedicated here to the unfinished work which they who fought here have thus far so nobly advanced. It is rather for us to be here dedicated to the great task remaining before us - that from these honored dead we take increased devotion to that cause for which they gave the last full measure of devotion - that we here highly resolve that these dead shall not have died in vain - that this nation, under God, shall have a new birth of freedom - and that government of the people, by the people, and for the people, shall not perish from the earth."[1]

I have personally visited the National Cemetery in Gettysburg and stood near the spot where President Lincoln delivered his address. It is impossible not to be humbled by the rows upon rows of Union dead.

It is incredibly difficult to imagine back to those dark days of the Civil War, picturing the President and the crowd all around him. Then to envision a woman, an unknown woman, coming to hear him speak and finding solace in his immortal words, with hope for her, the country, and his people.

The gravesite of Charlotte Georgiana Wickham Lee
the wife of William Fitzhugh Lee and
daughter-in-law of General Robert E. Lee.

Robert E. Lee III who only lived two years,
and his sister Charlotte Carter Lee
who only survived seven weeks.

Rooney's Wife

I am not so famous as my husband you see
History has faded me from sight
But that will not stop me to tell you my story
Of heartbreak, loss and plight
I came to the family of R.E. Lee was the name
And fell in love with the second son
'Tis William Henry Fitzhugh Lee
My life my joy my everything, God's will you see was done
My name I shall tell you, is Charlotte Wickham Lee
Of my short life I will now tell
Newlyweds in the Civil War, of such things that did dispel
From the first of our marriage I worried my heart
Of marches and battles and so
And deaths by scores with no end
My life my husband, please no
On a hot July day in the eighteen sixty-two
I buried our child, you see
Our beautiful boy was taken from Earth
Oh God, Oh God, help me please
And yet I continued on, expecting another babe
My heart became broken beyond compare
As soon she was to follow beside her brother
A little girl sweet, beautiful, and fair
Of these losses that cut my heart and took the light from my eyes
There was yet another agony, from which I could not arise
They told me you were captured by the North
And so was offered your bother in your stead
For you to come and be by my side
But it was refused and my heart again bled
There are such times in life, of this I tell you now
There is such a thing as death from a broken heart
It took me of this, I avow

Charlotte Wickham Lee

(1841-1863)

There is no photo of Charlotte Georgiana Wickham Lee that I could find, only her gravesite and that of her children. Her story is so moving and so heartbreaking it truly needs to be heard. While we know she is not nameless, she remains faceless in life and in death.

I came upon the tragic story of Charlotte while reading Mary P. Coulling's book, "The Lee Girls." The book follows the lives of Confederate General Robert E. Lee and his wife Mary Custis Lee with a concentration around their four daughters. In this book we hear about the obscure yet tragic life of Charlotte, the wife of General Lee's second son, General William Fitzhugh Lee.

A beautiful bride but a frail young woman, Charlotte gave birth to Robert E. Lee's first grandson, then later to a daughter. To her sorrow neither child survived. The son fell ill at two years old (1860-1862) and her daughter passed in infancy (1863). Her two pregnancies and the difficult effort of childbirth weakened Charlotte. The grief over the loss of her children, combined with her frail health seemed to break her spirit.

In addition, her husband who was the love of her life, was fighting for the Confederacy. She worried, greatly. Rooney (the nickname for General William Fitzhugh Lee) had been injured in battle, then imprisoned at Fort Lafayette in New York Harbor.

In late 1863, shortly before Christmas, young Charlotte's condition suddenly worsened. Rooney requested a 48 hour pass to visit his dying wife.

To appease the Union, Custis (William Fitzhugh's brother) volunteered to take Rooney's place in the prison. But Federal officials refused even the short 48 hour parole.

With no hope of seeing her husband again, Charlotte seemed to give up completely. She died on December 26, silently slipping into unconsciousness, her hands clasped upon her breast. She was only 22 years old. Family letters do not indicate the cause of her death (possibly tuberculosis or complications from her two pregnancies), but Robert E. Lee was notified at camp and he felt sure that his daughter-in-law had died of a broken heart.

Perhaps with modern medicine, young Charlotte would have been diagnosed with depression, perhaps also suffered from postpartum symptoms that negatively affected her health. She was also traumatized by her husband's capture, which sent her mental and emotional state into a downward spiral.

Conceivably, thousands of women during the Civil War undoubtably dealt with similar medical situations that in retrospect could be treated with today's medical advances. Unfortunately during Civil War times there was limited medical treatments for both emotional and physical health.

In her 5 ½ years of marriage Charlotte had thought about and cared for little else besides her children and Rooney. She was a devoted wife and mother.

General Lee's only consolation was that Charlotte had now "*joined her little cherubs & our angel Annie (the Lee's daughter Annie passed away on October 20,1862) in heaven!*"[1]

In this poem, "Rooney's Wife" we hear Charlotte speak of her losses and the deep love she felt for her husband.

It seems to me that the silent suffering and heartache so many women of the Civil War experienced was embodied in the short and sad life of Charlotte Wickham Lee. With that said, here she is given a voice to tell us about the love she felt for her husband and children.

Charlotte's memory lives on here, as a reminder to all, that not all casualties of the Civil War were upon the battlefield.

Clara Barton, from the National Park Service, Maryland

The Angel of the Battlefield

I will try to tell you as I see fit
The sights and sounds of battle
A place called Antietam I admit
Our Union men did so valiantly fight
I checked the date to see
September 17, of sixty-two or so it seemed to be
That led the corps of both North and South
To battle the Civil War
Into the cornfield we went, remains of those no more
Artillery fire into the field
Exploding at every side
Bullets flying and whistling by
Help me God I did cry!
I had not even bandages
To aid our bleeding men
I dragged them screaming and begging
God in Heaven I am at my end
And in the haze and confusion
Of that most horrid day
I saw a woman nearby the men
With bandages and water to aid
I ran to her then and called to hear her name
The noise about to great
Yet she stood beside us all
Heedless of her fate
And I watched her then so slight of frame
And watched a bullet pierce her sleeve
And killed her solider she was tending oh! Such a shame
The bottom of her dress had rings of blood
That weighed upon her feet

Yet in and all she did not stop
Determined to aid not sleep
As night fell on this most egregious of days
I asked a soldier or two
Who was that woman over there
The one that tended you
The ones that could speak shouted out to me
She is our Angel of the Battlefield from the Almighty you see
Her name we do not know nor do we care
She is an angel we cried, there is no despair

Clara Barton

(1821-1912)

In this poem, "The Angel of the Battlefield" we hear from an unknown soldier at the Battle of Antietam who fought on September 17, 1862 in Sharpsburg, Maryland. In the aftermath of battle the wounded soldiers are pleading with Clara to help them. The description of the selfless work Clara performed was given by Dr. James Dunn, a Union surgeon. "*In my feeble estimation, (Union) General McClellan, with all his laurels, sinks into insignificance beside the true heroine of the age, the angel of the battlefield.*"1

Even when a bullet passed through her sleeve and killed a soldier she was tending, Clara never ceased working. "*A ball had passed between my body and the right arm which supported him, cutting through the sleeve and passing through his chest from shoulder to shoulder. There was no more to be done for him and I left him to his rest. I have never mended that hole in my sleeve. I wonder if a soldier ever does mend a bullet hole in his coat?*" 2

She worked tirelessly, caring for sick and wounded soldiers throughout the Civil War. Clara Barton would later become the founder of the American Red Cross.

The Battle of Antietam (or Battle of Sharpsburg) claimed the most casualties in a *single day* of battle in the Civil War. In all, over 23,000 Union and Confederate soldiers were killed, missing or wounded in just over 12 hours of battle. The narrator of this poem says they do not know the name of the woman tending the soldiers, nor do they care, they only knew she was their angel, "The Angel of the Battlefield," Clara Barton.

The Angle
Gettysburg National Military Park

Site where Confederate General Lewis Armistead led his men
over the wall in a failed assault. They were overwhelmed
once they reached the Union cannons.

The Angle at Gettysburg

I raised my field glasses to take a look around
And spied the Rebels that were found
Across this open and expansive space
To where we know there was no grace
By the Union artillery that will surely sound
Of the din of battle that will certainly ground
All of those caught in between
The mighty, the meek and those unseen
So here I have come to Gettysburg is the name
To fight under Hancock under certain fame
And here I wait for the orders to come
To fire upon the Rebels, God's will be done
Yet as I spied across the field
I saw the flag that would yield
Of Picket's brigade I knew he was
The 9th Virginia and their cause
I prayed and prayed this day would never be
To raise my sword of one who is brother to me
You see he is the husband of my sister to state my case
A man I loved yet fear this fate
I promised my sister I would not fight
Against the man who loves with all his might
And now there is nothing I can do to stop this you see
The artillery is coming I am on my knee
Begging God to not let me see his face
In my line of fire beyond such haste
I hear the order to stand at the wall
And fire into their faces I see them fall
And oh, a Rebel is coming right for my heart
I raised my gun and without a start

Fired into the Rebel that came for me
He fell before me God help me please
For here at the stone wall it was overwrought
By a gallant number of Rebels as they fought
And met the Union fire without a thought
To the lives that were lost all for naught
And so as the blare of battle began to cease
This lost charge for the Rebels there is no peace
I noticed then the Rebel that had raised his fire
Was crawling to the stone wall it was so dire
I pulled him up past the wall and notice his face
My sister's husband I yearned to embrace
For I had promised her before I did fight
I would never raise my hand to her darling in might
For like a brother he was to me for all those years
I stood at their wedding I was beyond tears
And wondered to tell my dear sister of mine
Swollen with child as this war entwined
That it was I who fired the fatal blow
To the man who loved her so
And now I must live with the knowledge I say
It was I who killed her beloved that early July day

The Battle of Gettysburg

Confederate General Lewis Armistead
(1817-1863)

Union General Winfield Scott Hancock
(1824-1886)

It is well known there were instances of brother against brother fighting one another upon Civil War battlefields. One brother or friend fighting for the North and another fighting for the South. It must have been an unimaginable horror to face one another upon a field of battle. One such poignant instance is the story of two best friends, Confederate General Lewis Armistead and Union General Winfield Scott Hancock, who found themselves fighting one another on July 3, 1863.

Their friendship began following the Mexican War when Lewis Armistead was stationed on the western frontier. It was there that he met and befriended Pennsylvanian Winfield Scott Hancock. At the onset of the Civil War, Armistead chose to follow his state, North Carolina out of the Union and resigned his commission in the U.S. Army on May 26, 1861. This separation did not cause bitter or disagreeable feelings between the two friends, as they thought they would see each other after the war.

It was June 1861 in California the friends said goodbye to one another realizing one would fight for the Confederacy and the other for the Union. At the goodbye General Armistead said: *"Hancock you don't know how much this has cost me. If I ever raise my hand against you may God strike me dead."*[1] It was an evening wrought with farewells and tears for what lay ahead.

Two years later, on July 3, 1863 the war forced these two friends once again close, certainly not in the manner they wanted. General Armistead was one of General George Pickett's Brigade commanders. He would march along with 15,000 Confederate soldiers across the mile long and mile wide open field toward the center of the Union position. This failed assault at the hands of the Union would become known as Pickett's Charge. General Hancock was commanding the Union Second Corps. The Union position was centered at "The Angle" and was the focus of Pickett's assault. Some 1,500 Confederates breeched the wall and Hancock was wounded but insisted he not be removed from the field. General Armistead's brigade fought their way over the wall where he put his hat upon his sword and raising it shouting to his men, "turn this cannon, turn this cannon!" 2

General Armistead received three bullet wounds and succumbed to them two days later. General Hancock survived his wound.

Friend to Friend Masonic Memorial
Gettysburg National Military Park

The inspiration for this poem, "The Angle of Gettysburg" was born from the moment I stood at this very spot where approximately 1,500 Confederates stormed the Union line during the failed attempt at Picket's Charge.

History tells us the tragic story of Generals Armistead and Hancock, two best friends who found themselves on the field of battle against each other on July 3, 1863. Best of friends that the war forced into opposition and caused one of them to die at the hands of the other.

In the poem, "The Angle of Gettysburg" two unknown men related by marriage find themselves on opposite sides of the Civil War.

But what of those other husbands, brothers, fathers and friends who not only fought against one another, but who actually caused the death of the other? The lines of war divided families and friends. I have wondered over the course of the four long bloody years how many men and families dealt with similar situations.

In the poem, the Union soldier kills his expectant sister's husband, a Confederate soldier. This tragedy left the survivor to bear the guilt of killing his brother-in-law on the field of battle and bearing the shame of telling his sister the truth, that it was his own bullet that felled her husband.

I can almost hear and feel the suffering of the loss in the surviving soldier. His duty to the Union was complete, yet he will forever be morally and emotionally wounded, his heart in agony for the family he so dearly loved.

The dying Catalpa Tree at
Chatham Manor in Fredericksburg, Virginia
Author's own photo

The Catalpa Tree

I have stood at this very place
A hundred and eighty years in the same space
And now I will tell you of what I have seen
Over the years and in between
Chatham Manor is the name
Of where I have stood I do refrain
Of those I have witnessed and witnessed me the same
Names, faces that do reign
And tell you I saw Robert E Lee
Courting his dear Mary I do decree
Of times of joy that came and went
And times of despair when blood was spent
It was I say winter of sixty-two
A Civil War raged and I knew
That after the brutal guns that rained and fired
In Fredericksburg to the Rappahannock it was so dire
And so Clara Barton came to give aid
Along with Walt Whitman they could not save
And what I witnessed was so grievous I say
As the Union wounded came here, so how I prayed
Arms, legs discarded near me
Their blood life seeping to the earth you see
Forever now they are a part of this tree
For now I must tell you the time has come near
I am dying too, yet I have no fear
For all I have seen and witnessed you see
I now ascend to you all, you have waited for me

Walt Whitman

(1819-1892)

The great American poet, Walt Whitman, is not only remembered for his great literary works, but for his selfless and heartfelt services to his beloved Union.

In December 1862, the poet heard that his brother, Lieutenant George Whitman who was serving in the 51st New York was identified as one of the men who had been wounded at the Battle of Fredericksburg. Walt immediately journeyed to Fredericksburg from his home in New York in search of his brother George.

The search led him to Chatham Manor, where the Union Army had their headquarters, but his brother was not there. The news was that although his brother was wounded, it was only a slight facial wound. Walt gave up his search after hearing his brother was doing well and was back on the frontline.

However, the trip changed things for the poet. It was at Chatham Manor that Walt's own service to the Union Army began, as a nurse. The sights at the war hospital and the horrors that brought scores of dying men to Chatham moved the poet to write his book, "The Wound Dresser."

...*"began my visits (December 21, 1862) among the camp hospitals in the Army of the Potomac, under General Burnside. Spent a good part of the day in a large brick mansion [Chatham] on the banks of the Rappahannock, immediately opposite Fredericksburg. It is used as a hospital since the battle, and seems to have received only the worst cases. Outdoors, at the foot of a tree, within ten yards of the front of the house [probably the still standing Catalpa tree], I noticed a heap of amputated feet, legs, arms, hands, etc. -- about a load for a one-horse cart. Several*

dead bodies lie near, each covered with its brown woolen blanket.
In the dooryard, toward the river, are fresh graves, mostly of
officers, their names on pieces of barrel staves or broken board,
*stuck in the dirt"*1

The inspiration for this poem, "The Catalpa Tree" are the actual Catalpa trees themselves located at Chatham Manor which overlooks the Rappahannock River in Fredericksburg. The grounds and gardens at Chatham Manor are equally as beautiful, the view of the Rappahannock spellbinding.

The Manor itself was Union General Ambrose Burnside's headquarters during the Battle of Fredericksburg (December 12-15, 1862) in which 15,000 Union soldiers were killed at the stonewall at Marye's Heights. It was a total Confederate victory.

The Catalpa trees on the grounds of Chatham Manor stand in silent witness to the death that surrounded them so many years ago. In this poem the narrator is Mother Earth. She is the Catalpa tree standing in silent witness to her life over 180 years ago. She tells us of all she has seen and witnessed in her long life, the passing of time, of seasons, of joys and of sorrows. The Civil War was her sorrow; she is the living witness tree to the horror of that long ago War. The dying soldiers were all around her and became a part of her.

But these Catalpa trees will eventually die. Their witness to the past sufferings will end as well.

I have stood near and touched the Catalpa trees at Chatham Manor. They are now knarred and twisted with time. That is just the outside.

Inside is the heart, the heart of Mother Earth.

The Chancellorsville House

The location for the Battle of Chancellorsville

The Green and the Gold

I walked through the fields of green and gold
Of whose beauty it was to behold
And came upon the hyacinth you see
Colored like gems that beckoned to me
And stood beneath the dogwood in bloom
Whose pink petals would forever loom
And as I gazed upon the sky
Colored ice blue like thine eyes
Awash in perfection upon this scene
God's handiwork, the Almighty being
Yet for my heart there is no rest
For the war raging a sword in my breast
'Tis been three weeks now without a word
Certainly by now I would have heard
It was in Chancellorsville you wrote to me and said
Not to worry the Yankees had fled
Yet here I sit until now I just heard
A rider on horseback most assured
He came upon me with a note he did give
I fell to my knees I could not forgive
My eyes blinded with tears my hand numb with pain
I tore through the letter cried out in refrain
My God, my God you have taken thee
Into thine grace forever to be
Wait for me my love I will come soon
My life is over ne'er to bloom
For how can I can live without the sight
Of those ice blue eyes that haunted my life

Battle of Chancellorsville
April 30—May 6, 1863

In this poem, "The Green and the Gold" we hear from an unknown woman who is out walking the fields in springtime sensing the beauty of God all around her. Around her shines the glory of a beautiful day, yet she is worrying about her husband, the man she deeply loves. It has been three weeks without word, as she has not heard from him since the fighting began at the Battle of Chancellorsville.

The battle was fought from late April until early May 1863. It was General Robert E. Lee's greatest tactical victory over Union General Joseph Hooker's Army of the Potomac. Lee gained his victory by taking long chances. He did this by splitting his army, thus appearing to have greater numbers of soldiers when, in fact, he did not. This maneuver as well as a brilliant flanking military move by General Stonewall Jackson helped to ensure the Confederate victory.

The victory may have been Lee's greatest achievement, but it came with a great loss, the death of General Stonewall Jackson. This was a loss that Lee would never recover from for the rest of the Civil War.

The fatalities of soldiers for both the Union and the Confederacy were staggering. Approximately 17,000 Union soldiers were either killed, missing, or wounded and approximately 15,000 soldiers for the Confederacy.

Even with these sustained losses, the victory for General Lee was total. He believed his army was invincible. It was this mindset of invincibility that would invariably be his downfall, and that loss would soon come to fruition on a battlefield called Gettysburg.

Yet, in the beauty and serene setting of this poem, a rider on horseback approaches the unknown woman and hands her a letter. It declares the awful truth, that her beloved has died. She falls to her knees in despair and tells God to take her now.

One wonders how many similar letters were delivered to those families for both North and South, women on the home front waiting and worrying only to hear news of the death of their loved one. One also wonders how many at home simply gave up and died of a broken heart, unable to go on.

It may have been a Civil War, yet entwined within it are all the elements of a Shakespearean tragedy; one that tragically played out for four long bloody years.

The author Lisa G. Samia standing in front of the Klingel
House at sunset in Gettysburg National Military Park.
Author's own photo

The Klingel House

My eyes could barely see for the tears that stung my sight
News my son Ethan had ascended to the Almighty's light
The letter I held in my hand from your Commander I see
To tell me of your bravery so that others could be free
In early July of eighteen sixty three
Upon the battlefield of our North
Gettysburg 'tis the name
So how you did go forth
Three days of such fighting the slaughter I cannot grasp
So many gone like you my son, I fear I shall collapse
But as I read the letter and heard of how you died
It is as if I can see you my son and be there at your side
So now I will take my breath and read the part of your pain
And left this earth a better man of this I shall refrain
'Twas on July the 4th the holiday of our nation's birth
They found your body my son
With your comrade next to you
God's will you see was done
It says here you were wounded
And tried to take shelter I see
To the Klingel farm under the porch yet it was not meant to be
The owner came and found his farm littered with the dead
Of three days of the din of battle where the nation bled
I see you my son under that porch as you tried to save your life
Yet God had other plans for you and took you from that strife
There is no more to say just now the letter it ends with thanks
For the sacrifice of so many; my Ethan in the ranks

The Story of the Klingel House

Gettysburg, Pennsylvania

The Klingel House was purchased by Daniel Klingel in April of 1863 and he lived there with his wife Hannah and their two young children, Samuel and Catherine. Daniel's profession was a farmer and a shoemaker.

Little did Daniel and his family realize that in just three months the house would be surrounded, centered in the midst of the bloodiest days of fighting at the Battle of Gettysburg on July 2-3, 1863.

The morning of July 2 the family was warned by Union forces that they must leave their home. They vacated their property as per the warnings and headed by way of the Trostle farm to the base of Little Round Top.

It would be at the foot of Little Round Top that an assault by the Confederates would commence and invariably fail. Thousands of dead soldiers from both Union and Confederate would be the result of this assault.

On July 4, the Klingel family returned to their home to find a devastating scene. Bullet holes riddled the house and powder marks charred the walls from inside the house, where the soldiers had taken refuge to continue their fight. Crops were destroyed as well as most of the fences around their property.

"The farm was covered by the dead. Bodies lay all around the house. Two were just inside the gate, and two others under the porch where they must have crawled for shelter before dying of their wounds. One shattered tree in Klingel's orchard concealed four dead soldiers huddled around a cooking pan with food still in it."[1]

In this poem "The Klingel House" we hear the voice from an unknown woman, in this case a Northern mother, who received a letter from her son Ethan's commanding officer that he was killed during the Battle of Gettysburg. In it she realizes that after the battle, thousands of soldiers were lay dying or dead around the Klingel House.

The aftermath was horrifying as she learns that Ethan was found under the porch of the house with a comrade, perhaps trying to shield themselves from the battle.

I have visited the Klingel House and stood upon that very same small porch. From there the voice of this unknown woman comes to light to tell us of her son. We understand his great sacrifice and the pride she had in his death.

There is a palpable sadness that surrounds this house, silent and quietly heartbreaking. It is brought to life by this unknown mother and son bound together, forever in Gettysburg.

The Union Army entering Richmond April 3, 1865

The Last Days of Richmond

As I set to write this diary of mine
To tell you the truth of the dying time
Of the last days of Richmond at the end of the war
Where none of us were spared and all of us bore
Such sights and horror those days bring to mind
Of now I will tell you beyond the sublime
It was after President Davis heard from General Lee
Richmond was falling we had to flee
That the Rebel forces so few in number to defend
Set fire to the armory to leave nothing to lend
And so the fire it raged upon the citizens you see
My heart lurched at the story I will now bring to be
My husband's niece in Richmond she was
A beauty at eighteen it gave me pause
For stricken with typhoid sick in her bed
As her home around her burned and bled
The flames came and she was taken away
To die in the street I ask you to pray
And could do nothing as the fire spread
And barely could I save not even a thread
And one more story of yet a sweet young life
Whose story is true yet bathed in strife
So happy was she honestly I do state
The Yankees came there would be food to make
And so she went to see of their fare
Bread, cheese and nuts she did declare
And so it was the glee of the food that came to her view
To stave of the hunger that we all knew
She was so happy she could die she did state
Of this I will tell you was indeed her fate

Of these stories I tell you now they are true
The burning of Richmond and all we knew
And as I close this diary for now you see
The death and agony is all around me
I can only pray as we go forth
Healing has begun with the North
That we as a people will unite again
And God Almighty will bless his brethren

Words from The Wife
Of a Confederate Officer

In this poem, "The Last Days of Richmond" we hear from Myrta Lockett Avary's book entitled, "*A Virginia Girl in the Civil War by the wife of a Confederate Officer.*" The true harsh reality comes to us in vivid imagery during the last days of Richmond, when the citizens especially the women, were on their own.

"A niece of my husband's, a beautiful girl of eighteen, who had been ill with typhoid fever, had to be carried out of a burning house that night and laid on a cot in the street. She died in the street and I heard of other sick persons who died from the terror and exposure of that time.

I must tell of one person who did not weep because the Yankees had come. That was a little girl in the house who clapped her hands and danced all around.

"The Yankees have come! the Yankees have come!" she shouted, "and now we'll get something to eat. I'm going to have pickles and molasses and oranges and cheese and nuts and candy until I have a fit and die."

She soon made acquaintances next door. The soldiers or their servants gave her what she asked for. She stuffed herself with what they gave her, and that night she had a fit and died, as she had said in jest she would, poor little soul!

That afternoon there was a funeral from the house, and all day there were burials going on in Hollywood."[1]

How tragic are these two stories! Women were often casualties of the Civil War, just like the soldiers. Without a name or a face, we hear a voice brought forth from the silent past. Let us not forget them as we strive to understand their sorrow and embrace their sacrifice, from so many years ago.

Myrta Lockett Avary

The Reality of War

I shall tell you a story as plain as can be
Of a neighbor of sorts as best I can see
You see this here story is so heartbreaking I say
Beyond all the limits of God not even to pray
There was a young soldier from hereabouts he was
Handsome, genteel and fought for the cause
Just married he was in the summer of sixty two
Right here in Richmond for all who knew
And the bride was of the loveliest of face
Serene kind and full of grace
Lovely and noble they both were you see
'Till the Battle of Seven Pines came to be
The young bride heard of her husband's death
Then gave birth with her very last breath
For so bereft she was of both husband and child
She passed away too we were so wild
So instead of one grave
There were three I did see
For the young family we could not believe
All we could think of how the young mother passed
Death by a broken heart
Reunited at last

Myrta Lockett Avary

(1857-1946)
A Virginia Girl in the Civil War
by the wife of a Confederate Officer

In the diary, "*A Virginia Girl in the Civil War by the wife of a Confederate Officer*" the writer, Myrta Lockett Avary, records the story of her neighbor, who was the wife of a Confederate officer and her experiences during the Civil War.

While Myrta's personal writing took on a different tone, in this body of work she conveys the stories exactly as told to her, presenting them in the words of a woman who not only witnessed but suffered during the Civil War. As Myrta wrote in her introduction to the book:

"*This is the essential value of A Virginia Girl in the Civil War: it shows us simply, sincerely, and unconsciously what life meant to an American woman during the vital and formative period of American history.*"

The following excerpt is from the chapter titled the same as our poem where the woman has witnessed the battles raging at Seven Pines, near Richmond.

She has gone there to meet with her husband, who sent for her prior to the battles breaking out.

"*For two days it raged - for two days the booming of the cannon sounded in our ears and thundered at our hearts. Friends gathered at each other's houses and looked into each other's faces and held each other's hands, and listened for news from the field. And the sullen boom of the cannon broke in upon us, and we would start and shiver as if it had shot us, and sometimes the*

tears would come. But the bravest of us got so we could not weep.
We only sat in silence or spoke in low voices to each other and
rolled bandages and picked linen into lint. And in those two days
it seemed as if we forgot how to smile."

"Telegrams began to come; a woman would drop limp and
white into the arms of a friend—her husband was shot. Another
would sit with her hand on her heart in pallid silence until her
friends, crowding around her, spoke to her, tried to arouse her,
and then she would break into a cry:"

"O my son! my son!"

"There were some who could never be roused anymore; grief
had stunned and stupefied them forever, and a few there were
who died of grief. One young wife, who had just lost her baby and
whose husband perished in the fight, never lifted her head from
her pillow. When the funeral train brought him home we laid her
*in old Blandford beside him, the little baby between."*1

The inspiration for this poem, "The Reality of War" comes
directly from this factual event that was recorded through this
woman's eyes in the diary. We have no name for the young
woman who passed away, possibly from grief, nor do we know
the name of her child. They remain nameless and faceless, but
within this work have been given a voice to tell us of their
suffering.

There are moments and events of the Civil War that are
deeply sorrowful, this is one of them. It reaches out from
beyond the years, certainly the impact feels as mournful today
as it did all those years ago.

There are no verses of comfort that could be written to mask
this grief. In as much as the narrator of the poem tries to
embody that feeling; the words "reunited at last" are an attempt
to bring comfort for inconceivable grief.

Cornelia Peake McDonald

Winchester, Virginia 1862

I made my way past the front of my door
To where the earth was disturbed, just days before
And stood and gazed at the small square of earth
That housed my baby, two years after her birth
And as I knelt before the tiny grave
The tears falling that could not save
Her, from the early death
Baby girl come back, take my breath
And as I stared at the flowers that bloom
And surround you now in your earthly tomb
I heard a thunderous noise and raised my head
To see the swarm of soldier's our Johnny Reb
And wonder of wonder's it was ever so true!
Our daring leader Stonewall, and I knew
That soon our Winchester it was known
Would battle the Yankees for our home
It was then I saw the General come near
And saw my face flushed with tears
And stood with me beside my baby's grave
His eyes grieving he could not save
And reached for my hand with effortless grace
Saying he knew of the pain of which I faced
For so he too did lose a son
Born stillborn, he said God's will was done
I met his eyes so deeply colored blue
And knew of his pain it was so true
Watched in silence as he reached to embrace
The little violets around my baby's place
And told me gently as he turned to leave
"God is with her, do not grieve."

Cornelia Peake McDonald

(1822- 1909)

Cornelia Peake McDonald was a woman who lived in the town of Winchester, Virginia at the time of the Civil War. She went on to keep a diary of her experiences during the war entitled, "*A Diary with the Reminiscences of the War and Refugee Life in the Shenandoah Valley 1860-1865.*"

Her town of Winchester would change occupation from Confederate to Union a staggering 72 times. Her husband Angus joined the Confederacy leaving Cornelia and their nine children to try to survive in the most difficult of times.

Cornelia describes the fear and horror as the Union Army occupied her home moving her and her children to just one room. She writes of the daily struggle for food and the daily struggle to keep her children safe and well.

Cornelia's writings bring the horror of living through those trying days of the Civil War to light. She writes of one event in which Union officers, who occupied a neighbor's grand home in town, burned the home as they vacated the town.

She describes in vivid detail and horror as she witnessed her neighbor run into to the burning home, to the second floor, to retrieve her sleeping baby. Cornelia and her children would eventually flee their home and become refugees of the war. Her husband Angus became a Colonel in the Confederacy and would die on December 1, 1864.

The inspiration for the poem, "Winchester, Virginia 1862" comes from Cornelia, who wrote of her own suffering over the loss of her child, her baby daughter Bess. Her profound grief at her baby's death was so intense and heartbreaking it reached beyond the years as she wrote:

"One evening as the sun was going down I held her in my arms, and as she breathed out her little life her eyes were fixed in my face with the shadow of death over them. The children stood around sobbing. The little breast heaved and panted, one long sigh and all was still; her eyes still fixed in my face. Ah that fearful shadow! How I saw it flit over that lovely countenance, withering all its bloom and leaving its own ashen grey to remain forever."[1]

Cornelia also wrote that she saw Confederate General Stonewall Jackson one Sunday in town, deep in prayer at her church. General Jackson did have a presence in Winchester in 1862. Perhaps the General did stop to comfort an unknown grieving woman sometime over the course of the Civil War. A woman without a name or a face, but now with a voice, to share a moment of grief over the loss of a child.

A woman perhaps, just like Cornelia.

Epilogue

    This collection is about and for women. While in many of the poems there are incredible glimpses of grief and despair, there is throughout the collection a subliminal thread of hope. For even in the darkest of days during the Civil War and the incredible suffering of both sides, it is the strength and spirit of women that prevail.

    From Cathay Williams, the only Black woman to enlist in the United States Army, to Clara Barton the founder of the American Red Cross, these women and others like them rose beyond their circumstances and created a way to not just survive, but to overcome and thrive.

    This book is dedicated to these women and to my family's ancestor, Elvira Finch Moore, who found themselves embroiled in a great Civil War. They not only endured but poured the foundation of hope and fortitude for generations of women yet to come.

Acknowledgements

To my husband, Jim, whose support and love
has made all of this possible.

Andrea Loewenwarter, Historic Resources Specialist in the
Office of the Historic Resources in Fairfax City, Virginia and
the Site Manager of Historic Blenheim and the Civil War
Interpretive Center, a Union soldier graffiti site.

Historian/Author, Terry Alford—friend and supporter,
thank you.

Seharut Suankeow, Publicist & Media Strategist
for SS & Co. Media.

Leslie D. Stuart, Creative Director & Executive Editor for
Destiny Whispers Publishing, LLC.

Eric Swanson, Librettist for "EDWIN, The Story of Edwin
Booth" and co-author of the New York Times bestseller, the
"Joy of Living."

Jane Kosminsky, Artistic/Executive Director of Great Circle
Productions, Inc., and Faculty, The Julliard School.

The Edgar Allan Poe Museum in Richmond, Virginia.

The Dr. Samuel A. Mudd House Museum
in Waldorf, Maryland.

Terri Wilson, and Deb Key Mundair, who are members of
the Avon Historical Society, Avon, CT—in support and
friendship, thank you.

Meet the Author

www.LisaSamia.com
FB: Lisa G. Samia
Instagram: AuthorLisaSamia
Twitter: @LisaSamia
www.DestinyNovels.com

Lisa G. Samia

Author, Award Winning Poet & Speaker

"The Nameless and the Faceless of the Civil War" a collection of 28 poems and 28 essays was awarded Recipient of the 2020 Artist in Resident program through the National Parks Arts Foundation, NPS Gettysburg Poetry and was named FINALIST in 2018 & 2019.

"My Name is John Singer" and the sequel, "My Name is Mrs. John Singer" a fictional account of John Wilkes Booth.

"The Man with the Ice Blue Eyes," a collection of love poems debuted number one Amazon.com for Poetry for Women in July 2016. Two poems in the collection earned awards from the CT Authors and Publishers Association.

RJ Julia Independent Booksellers, Madison and Wesleyan, Middleton, CT.

Lecturer at Blenheim, Civil War Interpretive Center in Fairfax, VA.

The Doctor Samuel A. Mudd House Museum in Waldorf, MD.

The Edgar Allan Poe House Museum in Baltimore, MD. and the Poe Museum in Richmond, VA.

Guest lecture at the Civil War Round Table Congress, regarding "John Wilkes Booth, Son, Brother, Uncle and Actor" also lectures for "John Wilkes Booth & Asia Booth Clarke 'so runs the world away.'"

Endorsed by Great Circle Productions Inc. New York, NY.

Endorsed by Eric Swanson, the New York Times best-selling co-author of "The Joy of Living," and author of books & lyrics of "EDWIN, The Story of Edwin Booth."

Originally from Boston MA, Lisa now resides in Avon, CT. with her husband Jim.

Attended the University of Massachusetts in Boston.

Member of the following Historical Societies:

Ford's Theater, Washington, DC
Lincoln Cottage, Washington, DC
The Surratt Society, Clinton, MD
The Junius Brutus Booth Society (Tudor Hall), Bel Air, MD
The Civil War Trust
The Doctor Samuel A. Mudd Society, Waldorf MD
The Avon Historical Society, Avon, CT
Civil War Round Table, CT
The Poe Museum, Richmond, VA
The Poe House-Museum, Baltimore, MD
The American Civil War Museum, Richmond, VA
Society for Women and the Civil War
Civil War Round Table Congress

References & Historical Sources
Photos, Sources and Citations

Elvira Finch Moore
Photo: Carte de Visite of Elvira Finch Moore, undated image. Authors own family legacy property

All Ye of Gettysburg, Rise
Photo: view of Gettysburg from Seminary Ridge
Source:https://images.search.yahoo.com/yhs/search?p=public+domain+photos+of+gettysburg+after+the+battlewikimedia.org%2Fwikipedia%2Fcommons%2Fc%2Fc2%2FGettysburg_from_Seminary.jpg
1. Source: quote from Tillie Pierce -Source: https://en.wikipedia.org/wiki/Tillie_Pierce

Baileys' Crossroads
Photo: Family photo of Millard J. and Jesse Moore on their wedding day April, 1893. Author's own
1. Source: ThoughtCo.com https://www.thoughtco.com/julia-ward-howe-early-years-3529325
Citation: Lewis, Jone Johnson. "Julia Ward Howe Biography." ThoughtCo. https://www.thoughtco.com/julia-ward-howe-early-years-3529325 (accessed September 23, 2020).

Bread or Blood
Photo: Bread Riot in Richmond, Virginia April 2, 1863
Source: Wikipedia the free encyclopedia
https://en.wikipedia.org/wiki/Southern_bread_riots
1. Source: Katherine R. Titus, "The Richmond Bread Riot of 1863: Class, Race, and Gender in the UrbanConfederacy" https://cupola.gettysburg.edu/cgi/viewcontent.cgi?article=1019&context=gcjcweThe Gettysburg College Journal of the Civil War Era 2#6 (2011) pp. 86–146
2. Source: This eyewitness account appears in: Gallman, Matthew J., The Civil War Chronicle (2000) "Bread Riot in

Richmond,1863, "Eyewitness to History,
www.eyewitnesstohistry.com (2009)

Cathay Williams aka William Cathay

1. Source: https://www.nps.gov/people/cwilliams.htm
Photo 1: Cathay Williams Cathay Williams- Public domain
    image, Courtesy US National Archives
Photo 2 & 3 https://www.nps.gov/people/cwilliams.htm Artist
    William Jennings' fictional illustration of Cathay Williams.
    The monument to Williams located in Leavenworth, Texas,
    by Eddie Dixon

Cold Harbor, Virginia

Photo: The Garthwright House-Richmond VA site of Union
    Hospital -Battle of Cold Harbor June 1864
Source:https://stonesentinels.com/cold-harbor/tour-cold-
    harbor-battlefield/garthright-house/
1. Source: Hickman, Kennedy. "American Civil War and the
    Battle of Cold Harbor." ThoughtCo, Aug. 26, 2020,
    thoughtco.com/battle-of-cold-harbor-2360939
2. Source: historyplace.com
    http://www.historyplace.com/civilwar/

Columbia, South Carolina

Photo: The burning of Columbia, South Carolina, February 17,
    1865 / sketched by W. Waud.
Source: Waud, William, -1878, Artist. The burning of Columbia,
    South Carolina,/ sketched by W. Waud.
Columbia South Carolina United States, 1865. April 8.
    Photograph.
https://www.loc.gov/item/2003668338/.

Evergreen Cemetery

Photo: Elizabeth Thorn statue in Evergreen Cemetery
    Gettysburg PA
Source: America Comes Alive
    https://americacomesalive.com/elizabeth-thorn-1832-1907-
    six-months-pregnant-burying-dead-gettysburg/
1. Source: https://www.gettysburgdaily.com/elizabeth-thorn/

Ford's Theater

Photos: The view from behind President Lincoln's Chair in
    Ford's Theater Washington D.C., Author's own photo taken
    on location. Is this what Booth saw? Author's own
Presidential Box: Author's own

Have you seen my Caleb?
Photo: Gettysburg National Military Park in Gettysburg PA, the steps and trail leading to Big Round Top.
Author's own photo

In Thine Eyes
Photo: Library of Richmond Virginia, Civil War Research Guide https://www.lva.virginia.gov/public/guides/Civil-War/Women.htm
They Brought in Their Dead and Wounded on Hay Wagons, book illustration by Howard Pyle, Harper's Monthly Magazine, November 1904. Special Collections, Library of Virginia, Richmond, Va.
Photo and letter excerpt: https://www.nps.gov/articles/-my-very-dear-wife-the-last-letter-of-major-sullivan-ballou.htm

Janie Corbin
Photo: Find a Grave, database and images (https://www.findagrave.com : accessed 22 September 2020), memorial page for Janie Wellford Corbin (1857–17 Mar 1863), Find a Grave Memorial no. 10355261, citing Moss Neck Family Plantation, Moss Neck, Caroline County, Virginia, USA ; Maintained by Find A Grave .
https://www.findagrave.com/memorial/10355261/janie-wellford-corbin
Photo: The only known photo of Janie Wellford Corbin, added by John David Banta on 10 Mar, 2019.
Photo: Stonewall Jackson https://commons.wikimedia.org/wiki/File:Stonewall_Jackson_by_Routzahn,_1862.png
1. Source: History of American Women Stonewall & Anna: A Love Story https://www.womenhistoryblog.com/2016/06/stonewall-and-anna-a-love-story.html
NCPedia: Mary Anna Morrison Jackson
2. Source: https://en.wikisource.org/wiki/The_Dying_Words_of_Stonewall_Jackson

Jennie & Jack
Photo: Jack Skelly
Source: The Civil War Resource Engine Dickson College
"Skelly, Johnston Hastings," House Divided: The Civil War Research Engine at Dickinson College, http://hd.housedivided.dickinson.edu/node/40179.

Photo: Jennie Wade
Source: The Civil War Resource Engine Dickson College
"Wade, Mary Virginia," House Divided: The Civil War Research
Engine at Dickinson
College, http://hd.housedivided.dickinson.edu/node/40180
Photo: exterior door to The Jennie Wade House-bullet hole
Source: Author's own photo
Photo: The 1st floor bedroom of The Jennie Wade House
located in Gettysburg PA.
Source: Author's own photo

John – A Virginia Blacksmith
Photo: Illustration of John, a Virginia blacksmith, from a later
edition of "Hospital Sketches" by Louisa May Alcott
Source: "Hospital Sketches" from Wikipedia the free
encyclopedia
https://en.wikipedia.org/wiki/Hospital_Sketches
1. Source: "Hospital Sketches" by Louisa May Alcott (1832-
1888). Boston: James Redpath, Publisher, 221 Washington
Street, 1863. http://www.online-
literature.com/alcott/hospital-sketches/4/

Lorena
Photo/Sketch: Union Drummer Boy
Source: WP Clipart-A public Domain PNG image
https://wpclipart.com/American_History/civil_war/military/un
ion_drummer_boy.png.html
1. Source: the song "Lorena" on the Soundtrack for the movie
"The Searchers"
https://www.answers.com/Q/Is_the_song_Lorena_on_the_soun
dtrack_for_the_movie_The_Searchers
2. Source for lyrics:
https://en.wikipedia.org/wiki/Lorena_(song)

Mother Bickerdyke
Photo: From a Civil War Era Envelope. The New York Historical
Society/Getty Images
Photo: Civil War Talk, Mary Ann Bickerdyke
https://civilwartalk.com/threads/mary-ann-
bickerdyke.74603/
Source: Lewis, Jone Johnson. "Mary Ann Bickerdyke."
ThoughtCo. https://www.thoughtco.com/mary-ann-
bickerdyke-biography-3528676
(accessed November 1, 2020).

1. Citation: Ken Burns, "She Ranks Me," Textbook, accessed October 28, 2020, http://historymaking.org/textbook/items/show/250 Ken Burns, The Civil War (Arlington, Virginia: Public Broadcasting Service, 1990).
2. Source: Lewis, Jone Johnson. "Mary Ann Bickerdyke." ThoughtCo. https://www.thoughtco.com/mary-ann-bickerdyke-biography-3528676

(accessed November 1, 2020).

My Absalom

Photo: A daguerreotype of Mary Ann Holmes Booth dated between 1840 - 1860. Image Source: Library of Congress https://lincolnconspirators.com/picture-galleries/booth-family/mary-ann/mary-ann-holmes-dag-loc/
1. Source: Alford, Terry. "Fortune's Fool, The Life of John Wilkes Booth," Oxford University Press 2015 pg 14
2. Source: Alford, Terry. (edited) "John Wilkes Booth, A Sister's Memoir by Asia Booth Clarke" University Press of Mississippi 1996 pg 10
3. Source: Clarke, Asia Booth. Booth Memorials. Passages, Incidents and Anecdotes in the Life of Junius Brutus Booth, (the Elder.) (New York: Carleton, 1866) vii
4. Citation: Fairchild, Mary. "Meet Absalom, Rebellious Son of King David." Learn Religions. https://www.learnreligions.com/absalom-facts-4138309 (accessed September 22, 2020).

My Brother Johnny

Photo: John Wilkes Booth–unknown photographer
Source: This image is available from the United States Library of Congress's Prints and Photographs division under the digital ID cph.3a26098 https://commons.wikimedia.org/wiki/File:John_Wilkes_Booth_cph.3a26098.jpg
Photo: Asia Booth Clarke in the 1850's.
Source: from Wikipedia the free encyclopedia https://en.wikipedia.org/wiki/Asia_Booth_Clarke
1. Source: Alford, Terry (edited). "John Wilkes Booth A Sister's Memoir by Asia Booth Clarke" University of Mississippi Press 1996 pg 100

My Henry

Photo: from the National Cemetery at Gettysburg National Military Park in Gettysburg PA. Author's own photo

1. Source: Neely, Mark E. Jr. 1982. The Abraham Lincoln
   Encyclopedia. New York: Da Capo Press, Inc.
   https://www.nps.gov/liho/learn/historyculture/gettysburga
   ddress.htm

Rooney's Wife
Photo: The gravesite of Charlotte Georgiana Wickham Lee
Source: Find a Grave, photo added by Englishsunset
Find a Grave, database and images
   (https://www.findagrave.com : accessed 22 September
   2020), memorial page for Charlotte Georgiana Wickham Lee
   (1841–26 Dec 1863), Find a Grave Memorial no. 15437949,
   citing Shockoe Hill Cemetery, Richmond, Richmond City,
   Virginia, USA ; Maintained by Englishsunset
   (contributor 46804247) .
   https://www.findagrave.com/memorial/15438047/charlotte
   -carter-lee
Photo Source: Lee Family Archive, Family Papers & Letters
   https://leefamilyarchive.org/family-papers/letters/letters-
   1862
1. Source: Coulling, Mary. "The Lee Girls" John F Blair
   Publishing 1987 pg 132 & 133
2. Source: http://freepages.rootsweb.com/~jwickham/
genealogy/charlott.htm

The Angel of the Battlefield
Photo: Clara Barton at Antietam, National Park Service in
   Maryland
   https://www.nps.gov/anti/learn/historyculture/clarabarton.
   htm
1. Source: National Park Service Maryland - Clara Barton at
   Antietam
   https://www.nps.gov/anti/learn/historyculture/clarabarton.
   htm
2. Source: Lewis, Jone Johnson. "Clara Barton Quotes."
   ThoughtCo. https://www.thoughtco.com/clara-barton-
   quotes-3528483 (accessed January 28, 2021).

The Angle at Gettysburg
Photo: Union battery at The Angle facing the failed
   Confederate's Picket's Charge. Located on Gettysburg
   National Military Park in Gettysburg, PA.
Photo 1: courtesy of SS&Co. Media
Photo 2: Source https://gettysburg.stonesentinels.com/other-
   monuments/friend-to-friend-masonic-memorial/

1. Source: the Gettysburg Information Page
   http://djm1863.tripod.com/id2.html
2. Source: the Gettysburg Information Page
   http://djm1863.tripod.com/id2.html

The Catalpa Tree
Photo: The dying Catalpa Tree at Chatham Manor in
   Fredericksburg, Virginia. Author's own photo
1. Source: Walt Whitman at Chatham
   https://www.nps.gov/frsp/learn/historyculture/whitman.ht
   m

The Green and the Gold
Photos 1 & 2: Chancellorsville was not a town, but an
   intersection where the Chancellor family lived. A house was
   constructed about 1816 and occasionally functioned as an
   Inn for travelers on the busy Orange Turnpike. The building
   burned during the battle. The family rebuilt the house, but
   it burned in 1927. Archaeologists found and marked the
   outline of the original house.
   About mid-morning on May 3, General Joseph Hooker was
   standing on the porch of the Chancellor House when an
   incoming projectile struck a pillar which broke and knocked
   the general out. He regained his senses, but was forced to
   retire to the rear.
Source:
   :https://www.nps.gov/frsp/learn/photosmultimedia/chanhs
   .htm

The Klingel House
Photo: The author, Lisa G. Samia standing in front of the
   Klingel House at sunset. The Authors own photo, taken at
   Gettysburg National Military Park in Gettysburg PA.
1. Source: Gettysburg Stone Sentinels, the Klingel Farm at
   Gettysburg
   https://gettysburg.stonesentinels.com/battlefield-
   farms/klingle-farm/

The Last Days of Richmond
Photo: Union Army entering Richmond April 3, 1865
Source:
   https://www.flickr.com/photos/vcucommons/18491604209
   /
   https://commons.wikimedia.org/wiki/File:Union_Army_enterin
   g_Richmond,_April_3,_1865_(18491604209).jpg
Reference URL: dig.library.vcu.edu/u?/rpr,119

1. Source: Avary, Myrta Lockett. "A Virginia Girl in the Civil War"1861-1865 : being a record of the actual experiences of the wife of a Confederate officer https://archive.org/details/virginiagirlinciavary/page/368/mode/2up?q=369

The Reality of War
Photo: Myrta Lockett Avary
Source: Find a Grave, database and images
https://www.findagrave.com : accessed 29 October 2020), memorial page for Myrta Lockett Avary (7 Dec 1857–14 Feb 1946), Find a Grave Memorial no. 112785948, citing Oakland Cemetery, Atlanta, Fulton County, Georgia, USA ; Maintained by James Whitehead (contributor 48159843.)
1. Source: Avary, Myrta Lockett. "A Virginia Girl in the Civil War" 1861-1865 : being a record of the actual experiences of the wife of a Confederate officer https://archive.org/details/virginiagirlinciavary/page/40/mode/2up?q=369
Source: Documenting the American South, Electronic Edition https://docsouth.unc.edu/fpn/avary/avary.html

Winchester, Virginia 1862
Photo: Cornelia Peake McDonald
Source: Find a Grave, database and images
(https://www.findagrave.com : accessed 22 September 2020), memorial page for Cornelia Peake Peake McDonald (14 Jun 1822–11 Jan 1909), Find a Grave Memorial no. 18809342, citing Hollywood Cemetery, Richmond, Richmond City, Virginia, USA ; Maintained by JoAnne Peake (contributor 46980645).
https://www.findagrave.com/memorial/18809342/mcdonald
1. Source: "Entry by Cornelia Peake McDonald, September 26, 1862," House Divided: The Civil War Research Engine at Dickinson College, http://hd.housedivided.dickinson.edu/node/34728